# Wall Street Lady

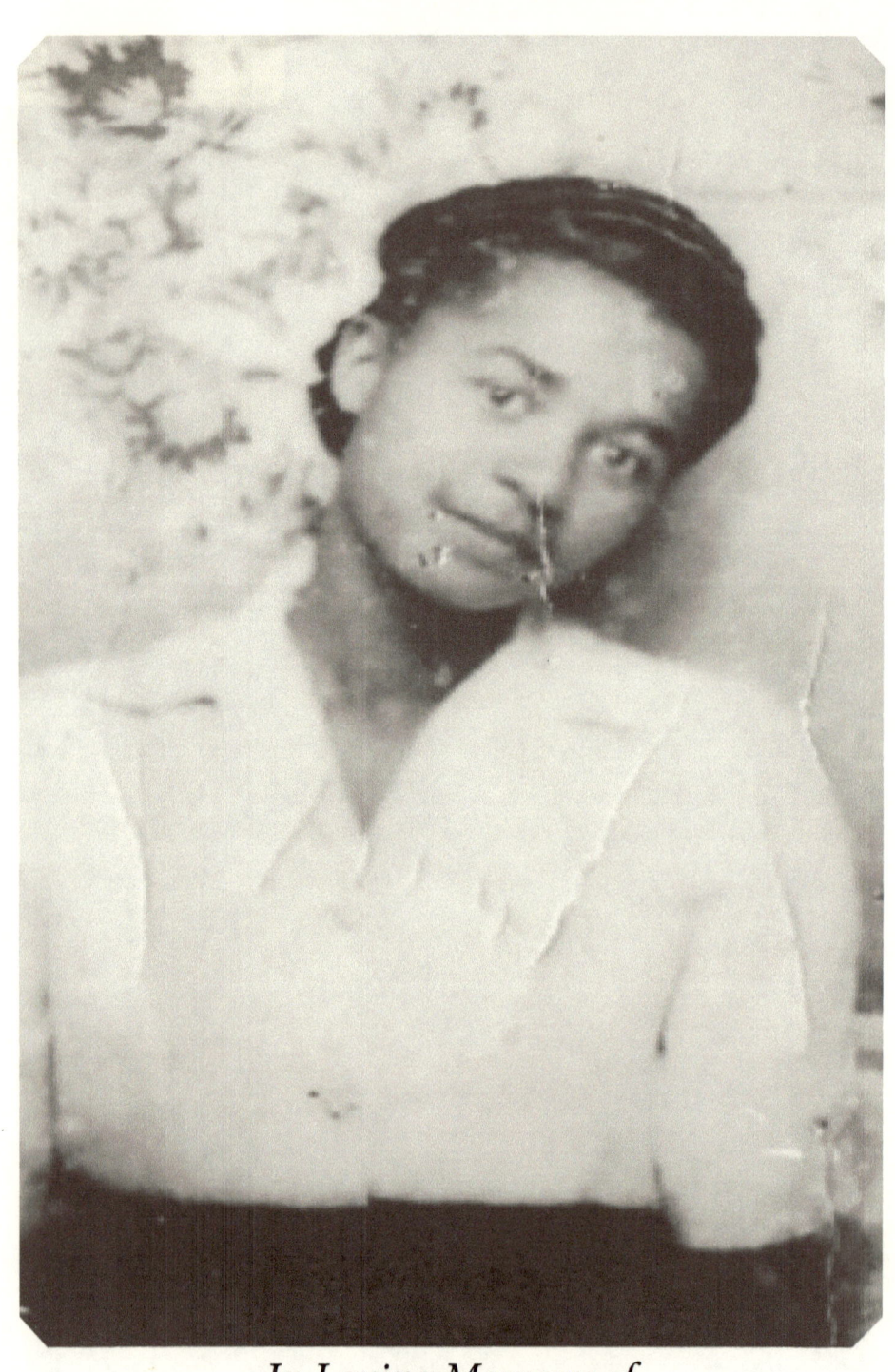

*In Loving Memory of*
*Willie Vernece Joyner Solomon*

# Wall Street Lady

The Inspiring Life of Willie Vernece Joyner Solomon

## Dolphine Solomon Lynch

 *Infinite Generations Publishing*

ISBN: 978-1-953364-10-4

Copyright © 2021 Infinite Generations

All rights reserved.
No part of this publication may be reproduced, distributed,
or transmitted in any form or by any means, including photocopying, recording, or other electronic
or mechanical methods, without the prior written permission of the publisher, except in the case of
brief quotations embodied in critical reviews and certain other noncommercial uses permitted by
copyright law. Cover design by I. Howard. Unless otherwise noted, all Scripture marked with quotations are from the Holy Bible, King James Version Copyright © 2016 by Thomas Nelson, a division
of HarperCollins Christian Publishing, Inc. Used by Permission.

For permission requests, write to the publisher, addressed "Attention: Permissions Coordinator," at the address below.

Produced and Published by Infinite Generations
137 National Plaza, Suite 300, National Harbor, MD 20745

www.infinitegenerations.com

# *Dedication*

*Honoring the parents God blessed me with to be their daughter, and the best siblings He sent to earth.*

*To my Husband, Jim, my partner in life; I love you.*

*To my four beautiful daughters, God blessed me with, I love you Sonya, Shelbie, Deanna, and Shauna.*

*To my wonderful, adorable grandchildren, I love you so much, Tyrell, Brittni, Kevin Jr., Destini, Ja'wan, Tiara, Se'vaughn, Paige, Drew, Alexandra, Khloe, and Kem (deceased).*

*To my precious wonderful great grandchildren, Charlee, Chase, Giovanni, Kash, Miles and all the ones that I have not met yet.*

# Contents

|     | Author's Note | ix |
| --- | --- | --- |
|     | Preface | xi |
| 1   | Philantha and Tilton's Family | 01 |
| 2   | The Girls Love Visiting Wall Street | 05 |
| 3   | Getting Ready for Easter Sunday | 11 |
| 4   | Ladies Quilting Party | 17 |
| 5   | Lang and Kyra's Night Out | 21 |
| 6   | Understanding Life | 25 |
| 7   | Lang Plans to Move Away | 29 |
| 8   | Kyra Meets the Love of Her Life | 33 |
| 9   | Brother Drives Lang to the City | 37 |
| 10  | Kyra's Attraction for Boone | 41 |
| 11  | Kyra and Boone's First Kiss | 47 |
| 12  | Life Changes Everyday | 51 |
| 13  | Bubba Visits Kyra | 57 |
| 14  | Kyra's Love Triangle | 61 |
| 15  | Lang Comes Home to Visit | 65 |
| 16  | Boone Joins the Navy | 69 |
| 17  | Family Time at the Fair | 73 |
| 18  | Kyra Receives Letter from Boone | 75 |
| 19  | Kyra Becomes Boone's Wife | 77 |
| 20  | Boone and Kyra's First Child | 81 |
| 21  | Birthday and Christmas Celebrations | 85 |
| 22  | Hope for a Son | 91 |
| 23  | The Family Grows | 95 |
| 24  | Boone and Kyra Move to the City | 101 |
| 25  | City Life | 105 |
| 26  | Tension Builds Between Kyra and Boone | 109 |
| 27  | Love Always Win | 115 |

# Author's Note

Readers may find the dialect of the book different from modern times. I have made every attempt to remain true to the time period, and to the voices of the individuals in this story. In order to do so, Chapters 1 and 2 serve as necessary foundation to understand Kyra's life in this era.

# *Preface*

I am Dolphine Lavern Solomon Lynch, daughter of Willie Vernece Joyner Solomon and James Ellison Solomon. I want my family to always be aware of how far we have come, where we originated, and the love that brought us forth. Life can start with love and end in pain, but true love will never die.

Wall Street Lady is about the life of my mother as a young lady at home with her parents and six siblings. In this book, Kyra is portrayed as my mother. I share to the best of my knowledge, the imaginations of her life on a farm with her mother and father in North Carolina.

Wall Street Lady depicts an era of Kyra's life. The Era of Black Wall Street, known for its majestic successes, growth, and shared community love.

Kyra is a young girl growing up on a farm, who meets the love of her life. She enjoys going to Wall Street shopping on Saturdays. Wall Street is a well-known street in Kyra's hometown that was for Black people to be serviced at salons, barbershops, and restaurants, as well as a place where young people socialized on weekends.

A majority of this book is based on a true-life story with some fiction. It brings out the true feeling of how love can blind, and at the same time, help heal the pains of life. Although it hurts; true love endures forever.

*In life, is it really the heart one should follow?*

# Chapter 1

# Philantha and Tilton's Family

It was a beautiful sunny day in June during the 1900s, the sun was hot and the house was quiet. It was eight o'clock in the morning, no one was home but Philantha and her daughter Lang. Philantha's name meant lover of flowers and seeker of truth. Lang's name meant one who talks and uplifts.

Philantha was now in labor, if this was a girl, Philantha had already decided to name her Kyra. Kyra, meant feminine lady and tender hearted. Lang was close to her mother's side because she was old enough to know something was not right.

"Mom, I will help you," said Lang.

"Mommy is good. I will ring the cow bell so Papa Tilton will come from the field." Tilton, which meant clover, blossom one of many fruits and seeds. "Tilton knows that three rings is the sign that I need you now," said Philantha.

Philantha gave birth to Kyra, a healthy baby girl. She was a pale little girl with puppy eyes and now they have two daughters. Lang was only two years old when baby Kyra was born. Philantha and Tilton loved children, and wanted to have a large family to help with the farm.

*****

Fifteen years passed as Philantha and Tilton raised their family on the farm.

Philantha called out from the kitchen, "Kyra! Why, are you taking so long to bring me the fresh water from the well?"

"I was combing my hair, making sure it looked perfect. I need new headbands, Mom."

"Kyra you do not need to look good to go outside to draw water."

"Oh Mom, you know how I am when it comes to my hair. I will always look my best at all times."

Kyra was only 15 years old at this time. Her mom was a hard worker and did not have much time to manage her daughters, Kyra and Lang's hair. Philantha had a beautiful head of dark coarse hair and she kept it pinned up most of the time. She taught Kyra and Lang how to comb and plait their own hair at an early age of six and to always be clean and orderly.

Philantha had to take care of six children, a husband, and the farm. This consumed most of her time, which she enjoyed. Kyra went outside to get the water. Skipping, something she loved to do, as she picked up the bucket from off the porch on her way to the well. She ran into her youngest brother Boe, coming from the field where he was with his Dad and brothers. Boe's name meant precious and honored.

"Hey Boe," Kyra said as she began drawing the water from the well, then she turned to him, "What's up Boe you look tired?"

"I am, we have this afternoon to finish the pasture that we are building for the mules. The old fence is falling down, so Papa wants to build a new one before the tobacco crop is in full bloom for harvest."

"We? You meant them, you are not building anything, you are just the errand boy, Boe."

"So why are you at the house? It is not noon."

"Mom and I have not finished dinner yet. Oh! Let me take Mom the water before I get in trouble again."

"Again? What did you do before Kyra?" asked Boe.

"Mom needed water and I was in my room combing my hair a little too long," Kyra said as she smiled and headed back towards the house.

"Ok sis, I know for the tenth time, right, you think you are a lady. See you later!" Boe said as he poured water from the bucket into his container and started running back to the field.

"See you later Boe," Kyra said as she skipped into the house with the water.

Philantha asked, "Kyra can you set the table while I make the Kool-Aid?"

"Yes, we have to plant some seeds in the garden this afternoon." Kyra skipped to the back porch saying, "Come in the house Lang. Come wash up for dinner."

Lang had been washing clothes all morning. She was outside washing clothes in a big black pot filled with hot boiling water. She had to stir the clothes around in the pot of soapy hot water with a big stick, rinse them and hang them on the clothesline. Philantha, made her soap from different ingredients molded and cut it up in pieces which the family used for baths, hair, dishes and the clothes; or for whatever needed to be cleaned.

Lang threw the stick down and said, "Girl, I was so hot in the sun and the steam coming from that pot made it worst. I am ready to sit down, cool off, and I am hungry."

Kyra looked into Lang's eyes as she took her by the hand, and they both went skipping along.

"I love you Lang, and I am so glad you are my sister. Can I plait your hair tonight before bed?"

"Yes girl, you love to style hair you need to be a hairdresser."

"No, when I grow up and get married I will have my own girls, and share my love for hair." They both laughed as they walked into the house together to finish preparing dinner with their mom. Kyra wanted to go check on her hair because it was so hot in the kitchen and she was sweating.

Her mom knew Kyra so well, that she looked at her and said, "Kyra, go get a scarf and tie your hair up before we go out to the garden after we all eat and clean up the kitchen."

"Thanks Mom, you are a Mom of wisdom. I love the way you have shown us how to conduct ourselves, and how to always look our best as young girls," replied Kyra. The girls were laughing and talking as they helped their mom finish preparing lunch.

Philantha said, "Girls, Papa and the boys should be here soon, it is 11:45 and they are due at 12:00. They only have an hour for lunch."

Kyra said, "Mom the table is ready."

"Kyra, let's ask our brothers what games we can play after supper tonight," said Lang.

"Hey Papa, hey boys!" said Kyra, as each one of them went straight to the water basin to wash their face and hands before they sat down to eat. Mom sat down and asked everyone to bow their heads to bless the food. There were beans, cabbage, cornbread and rabbit. Tilton was a man of few words, but the boys were loud and the girls listened.

Tilton said, "Ok, we will go back to work at 1:00."

"Yes Papa," replied the boys as they ate fast, so they could go lay on the porch in the cool breeze for a few moments and talk about their plans for Friday night.

Three were teens, Boe had to stay home with the girls. All of them could drive, only one was old enough to legally drive. Each one learned to drive the tractor at a very young age, around five. Kyra did not have the desire to drive, so her father never pushed her. Kyra had forgotten that her brothers would be going out because it was the weekend.

Kyra said, "Lang, it will have to be just me, you and Boe; but we are getting too old to play with Boe."

They laughed out loud. Kyra listened to the brothers as they talked about their plans for the night. Kyra called out, "Hey Brothers, Lang and I are old enough to spend time with you all. Boe is the only one that is not old enough, so we will ask Papa if it is ok for us to go to Wall Street with you all on the weekend."

"Kyra, you know what happened the last time you and Lang snuck out with us. We got in trouble with you two."

"I will wait another year and that is it for me," replied Lang. "Kyra, I will ask Papa. You remember when Papa got the gun and shot through the window to scare us for leaving without asking."

"Yes, he scared us good. He was drinking alcohol at that time in his life, but that period in his life is over," said Kyra.

"Yes, it is funny now how you, Kyra, had on new stockings being cute. I told you to wear some socks. I can see you now when you fell on that big tree stomp. You were more concerned about your stockings than your bleeding leg. I had on knee high socks and boots with my long skirt. So this time wear socks, so if you fall you will only get your socks dirty." They laughed out so loud that the boys wanted to know what was so funny. The girls told them about the time they went out and got in trouble, and now they were afraid to ask Papa again.

"He was drinking then, but he is still an overly protective dad toward his daughters," said one of the brothers.

They finished talking and everybody went back to their daily chores. Kyra, Philantha, and Lang, spent the afternoon planting tomatoes and squash in the vegetable garden.

Philantha said, "Girls, I have some flower plants to plant along the path out front." Philantha loved flowers and it showed when you came to the house. On each side of the house were beautiful flowers that bloomed all summer long around the house. There was a path with a big weeping willow tree on the front lawn. Philantha was a strong young woman that loved to sew, cook and plant flowers. Her background was of stern hard working women raised with no brothers, so living on a farm to her was hard labor like a man, she was a woman of wisdom and strength that was miss understood.

Tilton was concerned about his legacy. When he realized that his actions were not becoming of what his name stood for, he changed into a man of God. This gave him a purpose to help his family grow and be productive in this world for generations to come.

# *Chapter 2*

# The Girl's Love Visiting Wall Street

Kyra said, "Lang, let's go outside. Papa will be here soon to pick us up from Wall Street. The last time we came with our brothers I could not find you. I do not want Papa mad with me."

"Girl, I am not afraid of Papa, I am not afraid, but I love coming to Wall Street and dancing with you, my friends, and watching these handsome young men," Lang insisted. "Kyra, I think you have an eye for handsome men. The young men were asking me about you tonight."

"What did they say?"

"They asked if you had a boyfriend, how old you are, and said you could really dance." Kyra talked and enjoyed her sister more than anyone else. Kyra was so beautiful and so well dressed, that the young men were intimidated around her. Lang was pretty, elegant, tall and talkative, everyone knew Lang.

"Lang, tell your friends we will see them next week at the same spot," said Kyra.

"I can't next week, I am going to get my boyfriend to pick me up," answered Lang.

"We will see what Papa has to say about that," replied Kyra.

Over the next few months, Kyra and Lang enjoyed themselves at their favorite place, Wall Street. They thought their father was nice about giving them freedom and trusting them to ride with friends to Wall Street. Their brothers were ready to move on with their lives to the city. They were tired of farming, and having confrontations with their father after nights of partying. The oldest two brothers joined the Army. The third brother moved to the city with a distant cousin. Summer was coming to a close and the crops were harvested. The next school year was starting in a few days for Kyra and Lang. Kyra laid in bed late on a Saturday morning.

"Lang, I love high school, I am ready to return, and then I will have two years before I finish," said Kyra.

Lang said, "I am not returning; I am finished with school."

"What? Why?" asked Kyra.

Lang said, "I did not want to say anything, but I had to tell you first because you are my best friend for life, no matter how far we live apart. Kyra, I am pregnant."

Tears fell from Kyra's face as she said, "We will never grow apart Lang, I love you so much. What's next for you?"

Lang answered saying, "The last time Mom gave us rags for the month of our period, I did not need mine. Kyra, I also did not see that many rags used for the last couple of months."

Kyra looked at Lang, "What are you saying? Oh no, not me, then who?"

"Mom?"

They both laughed and then Kyra said, "No way, not Mom, that is so nasty."

Lang replied, "Kyra you are the one who told me, there is nothing wrong with a little nasty."

"You and Mom at the same time, wow! Well, whatever I love you, and I will help you with your baby whenever you need me." They hugged each other so tight, they fell asleep holding each other.

Later that night, Tilton walked in and found Philantha in the bed.

"Philantha are you feeling okay?" asked Tilton

"Well, I think I am with child."

Tilton smiled, "I could use another hand with me and Boe." Philantha poked Tilton in the side as they lay in the bed, smiling at him.

She said, "Really Tilton?"

"No Philantha, I am grateful and happy for any gift from God to our family." They shared until both of them fell asleep.

The next morning, Philantha called the girls in the room.

"Lang, are you sexually active?" asked Philantha.

"Mom? Why?"

"You have been sleeping more and gaining weight. Come here and let me look at the pulse beating on your neck. I already know, I just want you to know that I know." Lang fell on Kyra's shoulder and cried. Kyra just rubbed her arms and face.

Lang replied, "Mom, do not tell Papa."

"Girl, I told him first, he was disappointed and sad. What can we do now, but love the gift given to us from God? Every person is a gift, no matter how they were conceived. God is the giver of life. Girls, this is why I have been sewing more clothes."

Philantha pulled up her shirt and said, "Look, me too." They all cried, laughed, and prayed together that morning.

*****

A couple of month's later, Philantha gave birth to a baby boy and named him Rider. Rider's name meant great faith and travel by horse. Kyra's baby brother, Rider, was born on her 16th birthday. She loved to talk about how the baby was a gift and that nobody could have him because God chose him especially for us. After he was born they recited "Happy Birthday."

A few weeks later, Kyra woke up and saw Lang in pain. She ran through the house to find Philantha.

"Mom! Mom!"

"What Kyra?"

"Lang is in pain."

"Kyra, go tell the midwife across the street, Lang is ready." Kyra ran so hard, she fell a couple of times. She was scared, happy, and excited for Lang. Out of breath, she ran through the door of the midwife's home.

"Hurry, hurry, my sister is ready," Kyra said pulling her by her arm.

The midwife said, "Wait let me get my bag." Mom was home boiling water preparing for her first grandchild's birth. Kyra ran to Mom while the midwife was with Lang.

"Kyra, calm down and pray." She stood beside the bed and took Lang's hand and she squeezed Kyra's hand so tight. Kyra did not let go until her niece came out screaming. Lang, Kyra, and Philantha cried.

Kyra said, "She is a big bundle of joy, name her Polly."

"Rider will be so happy to have a playmate," said Philantha. She had Rider, her son, about three months before her first granddaughter Polly was born.

As Kyra was walking home from school with one of Lang's friends, she asked about Lang and told Kyra to tell her she was missed, and that she would be over to visit her soon. Skipping and then running home from school, Kyra could not wait to get through the door to see the babies. Lang was just finishing nursing Polly, while mom was nursing Rider.

"Too many breasts for my eyes," Kyra said thinking out loud as she began laughing.

"Okay since you are so jolly, come get your niece for a while," said Lang.

"No problem," replied Krya as she skipped over to Polly.

Philantha was preparing her list of food for the month and talking out loud at the same time saying, "We need flour, corn meal, lard, rice, and beans. I need lye to make more soap, but I do not need salt this month. Everything else we raise on the farm. I will leave Rider with Lang and Kyra when we go to town. The babies are toddlers now; they are getting older and need larger clothes. I have to stop at the fabric store."

Tilton replied, "You sure you're ready to leave them both with Lang? They are so busy now, they are more than a handful."

"Tilton, they both are responsible young ladies. It's time, I need a break, bring just Boe."

Kyra heard them talking, "These are not my children, I need a break too."

"Okay, you said Rider was yours."

"Well not on Saturday, I want to go to town. You know it will be another month before we shop again."

"Who said you were shopping Kyra?"

"Papa always takes me to the five and dime to get something for my hair. We sneak out while you are looking at fabric, and you never miss us Mom."

"Let's talk to Lang and see if she can handle both, then you can come with us." Saturday morning after breakfast, and the house was clean, they all prepared to head out.

Papa said, "Everybody in the car, I am ready." Kyra never left home until her bed was fixed. Sharing the bedroom was not easy with Lang, and now a baby.

Mom called out, "Kyra, you coming?"

Running to the car, "Yes, I had to wait until Lang got all those extra clothes off her bed before I could fix her bed and mine."

She turned calling out to Lang, "Be back later, Boe is with us." They arrived in town, and Philantha went into the store.

"I need blue and pink fabric for the toddlers and yellow for my daughters," Philantha talked with the retailer.

"Ok, you had twins?" asked the retailer.

"Well, you could say that, my son and granddaughter are a few months apart," said Philantha. This was the first day on the job for this retailer, so she did not know Philantha's story.

"That happened with my mom and sister years ago, and my niece lived with us until she moved away after high school. She is more like a sister to me than a niece."

"Your sister did not want her child with her I suppose, that was a hard decision for your mom and your sister."

The retailer answered, "Yes it was, but my niece was so young when my sister left home to find a job. When she came back, my niece was old enough to say no; she was around 5-6 years old. She would visit her mom in the city, but never could get accustom to being away from her grandmom."

Philantha finished shopping and went back to the car, "I am ready to go home and check on the babies."

"Me too Mom, I really did miss my babies." Looking out the window smiling because she had some royal crown hair dressing and some headbands for her hair. "This has been a great day Mom, and thanks Papa, you are the best Papa in the world."

They arrived home, and Lang was sitting beside the bed rocking both babies. Rider ate his oatmeal, but he looked at Kyra like he wanted to say that my mom always gives me milk when I finish eating. Laughing, mom took Rider from Lang. Kyra reached for Polly to give her a hug and kiss, and then looked at Lang.

"Lang, I went to the five and dime store. I got some hair grease for our hair, so I will help you to relax, as I comb your hair. Plus, I have some new headbands. The package came with four, two for me and two for you."

When Kyra went to school on Monday, her mom had made her a dress that matched her new headbands. Philantha could make a few items of clothing overnight.

Coming in from school, Kyra said, "Mom, my friends loved my new dress, and especially my headband. Can you make me a blue dress to wear when I go on my date? I have a few prospects."

"You are playing Kyra, for real?" asked Philantha.

"Yes, because you look like the sunshine today girl," added Lang.

Kyra smiled and asked, "Lang your new blouse is pretty. You like it?"

"I like anything Mom makes for me," replied Lang.

"Lang and I will be double dating Friday night, we are meeting two young men."

"Is this Polly's father?" asked Philantha.

Lang said, "No, that relationship did not work out, so I decided to move on."

"Well, that is the best decision when you know what you want. Then you will not settle for what you do not want."

"I know what I want, dark and handsome, big heart, big smile, and one that loves himself some Kyra."

"Where are you all going?" asked Philantha.

"Papa will drop us off at my favorite place, Wall Street. We will meet the guys, they will bring us home. We are going to shut the club down, it's Friday, Mom." She laughed and her mom laughed with her.

"Is there anywhere else you like spending your time doing?"

"Yes dancing is my number one thing, but I love school, church, and time with you, Mom, and Papa."

# Chapter 3

# Getting Ready for Easter Sunday

Kyra said, "I am enjoying myself, how about you Lang?"

"I am enjoying my date with this young man, he is very kind, and a great kisser," answered Lang.

"What already?" said Kyra.

"Yes, girl it was just a peck, but it was smooth," replied Lang.

"I think, I will wait until next week before I get my peck," said Kyra.

"Nothing like a good peck. Ha ha, let's get back on the floor and dance. It is getting late, I do not know how you dance all night," said Lang.

"Music gives me this feeling that brings so much energy to my soul. I just give in to the stirring in my heart and then I move to the flow of the sound," answered Kyra.

"I like to dance too, but I see it is a love for you Kyra," said Lang. They danced some more then left with their dates, headed home. Once they got home, Kyra and Lang stayed up and talked about their dates. They had to talk low and use a flashlight so they would not wake up Polly who was sleep in her bed.

"When we got to the path to turn into our house tonight, my date leaned in, and I leaned in too, and my peck was sweet. Thanks I will always trust you," said Kyra.

"I thought you said next week, really Kyra?" replied Lang. They continued to talk until they fell asleep.

The next morning, Polly called out from the back door, "Aunt Kyra, Rider and I have something to show you, look we went to the hen house with grandmom this morning and I have three eggs. Mom said we can paint our eggs for the Easter egg hunt after church so that we will have them for Easter Monday."

"Great I will check tomorrow for more to add to the ones you have, because Mom's sisters, and our cousins, will be with us at our house this year.

So we have to go into town to shop for new shoes, socks, and hats for us girls to wear with our Easter dresses," replied Kyra.

"The dress that Grandmom is still sewing on in the back room?" asked Polly.

"Yes, let's go see if she needs some help with anything." They walked in the back. "Mom, can we assist you or bring you something to drink?" asked Kyra.

"No, I have to stop, I am finished sewing for today. Let's get Tilton and head to town, " replied Philantha. They all got in the car, and drove into town. They shopped for a while and Philantha had two more stops in town. Tilton realized Philantha was still shopping.

"What's taking you so long today?"

"You know how people shop for Easter Tilton. I cannot find shoes for Rider, so I have to go to the last store and pray that they will have his size."

"Did you finish the grocery list?"

"Yes, I did. I have one more stop at my favorite place to purchase some block cheese from Cook's."

Lang and Kyra were in the car waiting for their parents. "Here they come," said Lang.

Polly was tightly hugging the bag with her black shiny patent leather shoes and ruffle socks. Rider jumped in the car beside Polly, telling them he had new shoes also. They were laughing and playing in the back seat during the ride home from town.

Boe, Rider's older brother, that was still home was in the front with Mom and Dad. He was the quiet one who loved to read, so they would always buy him comic books from the five and dime.

Lang said, "Kyra we have two big days ahead to prepare for Easter and help Mom."

"Great Lang, I love celebrating Easter." Everyone was up early for Easter Sunday. After breakfast, they all got in the car but Lang.

"Here I come," said Lang as she made it to the car.

"You okay?" Mom asked.

"Something about breakfast did not agree with my stomach."

"Here is a mint this will help"

"Thanks Mom."

After church was over they all went home to change clothes for the Easter egg hunt. Philantha was undressing when Tilton walked in the room.

"I know that look lady of wisdom, what is on your mind?"

Philantha answered, "Lang, is with child again."

"Are you sure?"

"Lang was conceived in the hardest stage of our marriage. I was young, and you were young. My outlets were cooking and sewing; and yours were working and drinking. Our communication skills were not good at all. Your goal was to make sure you could provide for me as a young wife and you have Tilton. I see how Lang has a hard time with communication when it comes to her feelings with us. I am so glad she has Kyra, I pray that she finds her happy place in life, in herself, and not a man. Tilton, change your clothes while I prepare supper for after the Easter egg hunt," said Philantha.

"One, Two, Three Go!!" The kids were falling and laughing as they were hunting for the eggs all over the front lawn, down the path and under the big weeping willow tree. Across the path beside the walnut tree, Kyra and Lang were hunting also.

Lang shared with Kyra, "I love you sister, we will always be alright because we have each other to live this life, and you were chosen for me and me for you."

The older young men were home for Easter, and they were hiding the eggs. Rider was glad that his three older brothers were there to share some of his stories he had read. Rider chose to play with balls more than listening to Boe's stories. The brothers were leaving after dinner, but since Tilton's Birthday was in a few days and everybody was home they decided to celebrate with him. Tilton did not like attention on himself, but he agreed. Tilton loved chocolate cake and the birthday dinner was beef stew, cabbage, cornbread, boiled potatoes, and barbeque chicken with a coco chocolate cake for dessert.

"Great dinner, thanks Mom," the boys said at the same time.

"We miss the good home cooked meals," said one brother.

"So let us all go outside so we can get a picture before you all leave."

Philantha hated to see them leave. She went in the bedroom, and got her pouch, put it in her pocket after she took out her snuff box and poured snuff in her bottom lip. She placed the money the boys had given her in the money pouch between her breasts. She had large breast where she kept her important items, like keys and money. Snuff brought her pleasure, and relief from stressful times.

Kyra said, "Lang I enjoyed the brothers, it is nothing like family time."

"So true," replied Lang. Lang was growing fast with child and Kyra was getting ready for graduation.

*****

Lang had another baby girl and named her Ammy, who Polly and Rider fussed over.

"Polly you always get to feed Ammy," said Rider.

"Yes, I am a girl that knows how to take good care of a baby," answered Polly.

"I am a boy that knows how to feed a baby too."

"Thanks for both of you helping, I have an idea," said Lang. She wrote out a schedule of which one would feed the baby after she nursed. Ammy had a big smile that brighten up her big eyes. In a few weeks, they forgot all about feeding Ammy. It was almost time for Kyra's high school graduation.

"Kyra, after your graduation, can we plan a birthday dinner together?" Philantha and Tilton were sitting outside under the large oak tree in the front yard.

"Tilton, I am proud of Kyra she is the first to graduate high school. That is a great accomplishment for her," said Philantha. A few days later, Kyra graduated and everyone celebrated and congratulated her.

Everyone said, "Congratulations! Congratulations Kyra!"

"Thanks everyone I am happy to have completed this stage of my life." They ate cake and then Kyra and Lang got ready to go out.

"Mom's cake was as delicious as always," said Lang as she changed her clothes. They finished changing then went to tell Mom.

"I am going out tonight to celebrate with some friends."

"Who are you riding with Kyra?" asked Philantha.

"Lizzie, Cousin Bee's daughter, has her license; I am riding with her to Wall Street tonight. Lang, I have my eyes on this young man. I asked this young lady last week if she knew his name and she said his name is Boone. Everybody calls him 'Good' because he is good to look on."

"Next time point him out to me Kyra, I think I know who you are talking about because he has another handsome brother that loves the ladies and they love him. He is a dancer," said Lang.

"You danced with him before," said Kyra.

"That is nothing new, I dance with whoever wants to move with the music and me," said Lang.

"Lang, you will talk with anyone, I like that about you," replied Kyra.

"Yes, it helps me concentrate on others and not think so much about me," said Lang.

"You have a heart for people Lang," replied Kyra.

*****

Next Saturday, when Papa and Kyra were on their way to town, he stopped the car on the side of the road where this young man was walking.

Tilton asked, "Do you need a ride?"

He said, "No sir, I am almost at my grandmother's house thanks." As he turned into the path Kyra smiled and he smiled, it was Boone.

Papa said, "Kyra you smiled like you knew the young man."

"No, not yet sir."

"Yet?" Papa replied.

"But I want to know him. Papa, look at those dimples."

"Girl, his father and I trade seed for our crops sometimes. They seem to be good people."

"Okay, so the next time you meet his dad, can I go?"

"No girl, this is grown folks business, in time you will meet him. I always want the best for my girls."

"Thanks, I love you." Tilton would just nod his head. They arrived home and everyone was waiting to tell him about the opening of the fair.

"Tilton, The fairgrounds opened today, that means two weeks of family and friends coming together with lots of food, games, music and gifts," said Philantha.

"I will have to drive the truck because it is too many for one car."

"I can ride with my friends, his dad will pick me up if it is okay Papa," said Boe.

"Who is his people?" asked Tilton.

"He is one of the younger sons of the man you trade seeds with," said Boe.

"Okay sounds good, I can drive the car then," replied Tilton.

"Lang, I will take turns with the kids so that you can enjoy the rides at the fair," said Philantha. After talking, they all decided to go to the fair. Boe rode with his friends, and everybody else rode with Tilton in the car.

"I am not riding; I can watch the stroller and Papa can hold Polly and Rider hands when they are not riding. I am going to get us candy apples, ready kids?" asked Philantha as she walked to the food stall. She asked for four candy apples and a cotton candy for Ammy.

"I want both" said, Polly and Rider.

"No, you all can share the cotton candy with Ammy. She only needs a little piece." Philantha and the kids walked back, eating their candy, to watch Tilton throw balls to win a teddy bear.

"Throw it again Papa," said Ammy. The bear dropped off of the wall where all the other bears were hanging.

"You are one strong man Tilton," said Philantha.

Rider asked, "Mom, you want the bear, that's why you said that right?"

"Boy," replied Philantha as she smiled.

Meanwhile, Kyra and Lang rode on every ride at the fair and then sat down to eat hotdogs, popcorn, and peanuts.

"I am saving some of my popcorn and peanuts to take home."

Kyra said, "Look Lang, Ammy's dad!" He came over to where they were sitting with another young lady.

Lang said, "Did not know I would see you here, I thought you had moved away"

"Yes, I came home to see my mother. I saw your dad with your baby, but I was scared to approach him. How are you doing?"

"I am good, baby good, and will always be good. Please leave our space."

"Lang, he said your baby," replied Kyra.

"Yes, she is my baby leave it at that. Change the subject. You want to win a gift for the kids?" asked Lang.

Two young men approached them, and said, "Ladies want to go on a ride with us?"

They looked at each other and replied, "We would love to ride with you." They rode the rides, played games with lots of laughter, then exchanged names.

"Thanks, we will keep in touch. Hope to see you all soon ladies."

On the ride home everybody was asleep but Tilton and Philantha. There were teddy bears everywhere in the car. Everybody got out of the car and thanked Papa. They all had a ball.

Papa said, "You all are welcome, and I enjoyed myself too."

Papa told Rider and Boe to bring all the stuffed animals in the house. Kyra woke up wanting to know where the pictures of Rider, Ammy and Polly were. Kyra said, "All three of them look so much alike.

Mom said, "Yes, strong genes and a great bloodline of people."

"I want to make a scrapbook of all the pictures we took today," replied Kyra.

Mom said, "Here is one of myself and Tilton."

Kyra replied, "Just add the one of us and not the young men that we were with. We do not what to look back years later and say why did we add strangers to our family collage."

"I will not Lang, you know how I love photos of the family. We need great memories for the future generations so they will see their heritage in print. Boe, the photographer in the family, said he will ask for a new Polaroid camera next Christmas."

# Chapter 4

# Ladies Quilting Party

"Ladies! I am so glad to see you all. I have tea to drink, hot or cold. I prepared some ham biscuits, fatback biscuits, tomato biscuits; and for dessert sweet potato jacks and plain sweet potatoes. Before we start quilting you all help yourselves."

Each lady had the colors for the side that they worked from. It was six ladies, and they were crafting a large quilt for a newlywed in the family. They had bright colors for peace and happiness. Philantha, has one cousin who seemed to be the one to start the conversations that a few dared to speak about. Husbands, and sex were their main topics.

"Ladies, I am so thankful for each one of you at this time, open up and feel free to express your thoughts, encourage someone, this is a time to share and release. We have no snitchers in this room." Cousin Bee was having problems in her marriage with communication. "So when you have sex, does he say anything?" asked Cousin Bee.

"No, he just say baby that was good." They all laughed.

She replied, "Well that is your open door to continue say, 'So glad you feel better because you were so quiet, I did not know.' After sex is a time to get him to talk about things you could not ask before, try it. And if he says nothing the next time you get in bed and if he makes the move, look at him and say, can I have relief and release."

"What does that mean?" asked one of the ladies.

Cousin Bee said, "As wives, as a wife we need relief in our souls, (whatever your concern is) and then we both can have a release together for the body and mind."

"Girl, majority of men will turn over in the bed and say goodnight."

"True, but not for those nights when you say no to them," replied Cousin Bee.

They were all laughing out loud and one of the ladies said, "Not sure of trying that one myself."

*17*

Philantha and the ladies worked for about four hours. Philantha was thinking they could finish the quilt within two more days together. The quilt was large enough to hang down like a spread on the couple's bed. Philantha felt that because the wedding day was in four months, and their lives was so busy, she wanted to finish a month before.

One lady said, "Yes, because I am working on a small quilt for myself, and my fingers cramp sometimes." They all understood, and would plan for another quilting party in two weeks.

Philantha replied, "I love these times together ladies, next time Cousin Bee, we will come to your house."

"That is good with me," answered Cousin Bee. They prayed for each other and their families hugged, and everybody went home. They all lived down the road and across from each other, which was in walking distance, just a few miles apart.

Kyra asked, "Mom, what time you need us to help you with supper? Lang and I are going for a walk down the road to our friend's house with the kids; we ate all the leftovers from breakfast for dinner, because those ham biscuits looked so delicious."

"Kyra, I made sure I cooked enough so I just have to warm some soup to serve with the ham, fatback, and tomato biscuits, plenty of sweet potatoes leftover."

"Mom, how much did you cook?"

"Enough to feed my family and the ladies. So you all come back by 3:30." It was still early, 12:30. Quilting always started right after breakfast which was around 8am. Polly and Ammy had their nap.

Rider said, " I am too old to nap.

"I am not too old for a nap," replied Ammy. She was up playing with dolls before breakfast at 6:30.

"Ammy always loved the smell of the red clay dirt hills along the road, look at her she has some in her hands," said Lang.

"Maybe because of you had a desire to eat red clay dirt when you were pregnant with her," replied Kyra.

"A majority of pregnant women eat starch from the box," said Lang.

"Starch? That is some weird craving. When they are not pregnant, they want snuff, not for me. Why are the girls bringing Easter baskets with us?" asked Kyra.

"They asked me if they could pick pecans for Grandmom so on our way back home, we can stop at the pecan tree," Lang said.

"Cousin Bee sent you two apple pies, and we picked pecans so you can bake pecan pies for Papa."

"Think you all can shell them for me?" asked Philantha.

"Yes Mom."

Papa just walked in the house and was headed to the sink to wash his hands when he said, "Something smells good."

Ammy asked, "Papa, you can smell my clay?" She had put some clay dirt in her pocket.

Papa laughed, "No, Ammy, I smell pie." He sat down at the table and Ammy sat on his lap.

"Papa I picked pecans off the ground today so grandmom can bake you your favorite pie."

"Thank you little one." She jumped down and called out to Polly. Polly was looking for Rider.

"Rider and Boe went to the creek to fish; they are due home now. Come help with setting the table, the soup is warm and fresh biscuits are in the oven." Philantha was pouring the soup into this beautiful ceramic brown bowl with two pink rings around it and one blue ring in the middle of the pink rings at the top of the bowl. Her mom gave it to her when she got married.

"Grandmom, I love this bowl."

She told her the story and Polly wanted to know why she was not allowed to clean the bowl. Grandmom told her that those little hands may drop the bowl and she just allowed her mom and aunt to clean the bowl. Grandmom also mentioned to her that the bowl was special and she wanted to use the bowl, but protect it at the same time for future generations. This will show how far we have come and the hardness of this bowl will prove no matter how much wear and tear we have in our lives, we can always stand the storms. Families need items, places, or things, to mark as memorial of their family value. One day, far into the future, this bowl will continue to shine in the home of my grands and great grands. It will remind them of the connections in the family.

Rider ran through the door with a string of fish. Boe was putting the fishing gear on the back porch that he and Rider made with poles, hooks, and wire on the end of the string. He put the gear in a safe place for their next trip to the creek to fish.

"Rider! You are as wet as the fish," said Polly.

"Boe and I went for a swim to cool off after we caught these fish for Mom to cook," said Rider.

Boe said, "Rider put them on the back porch, and I will clean them and put them on ice to cook tomorrow."

Washing his hands with Boe, Rider said, "We have at least twelve fish. This was a good day of fun. Let's go eat, I am hungry."

"Thanks for supper Philantha, Bee's pie was almost as good as yours."

"It was very tasty Tilton, she's always giving me something to show love for me just like you. Sometimes I think of her as my aunt and not a cousin, until we come together and act like young girls. She is so much more mature for her age as she is just two years older than I am. When Cousin Bee was still a child, she had to help raise her siblings with her father. Her mom had polio, she had problems walking so Bee had to help take care of four siblings and could not attend school.

"I am so glad she has a great husband that loves and supports her. She is so creative, and is the reason I am a seamstress now. Her twins and Kyra graduated at the same time with honors. We have intelligent genes, in our blood and prayer helps bring intelligence to the brain," said Philantha.

All the children were outside on the front porch playing games. Lang and Kyra were finishing the dishes.

Lang said, "During Easter when our brothers were here, I asked them to look for me a job up north with him. He told me that I could stay in the same rooming house where he lives, so I am preparing to move soon. I will talk with mom, because she already said Polly and Ammy will always stay here with her."

"I will continue to be their aunt while helping Mom in any way until I leave home," replied Kyra.

# Chapter 5

# Lang and Kyra's Night Out

I have this white blouse and black skirt that I want to wear to Wall Street on Saturday night, one of the band members will be celebrating his birthday. There will be pictures taken, for a small fee, if anyone wants pictures," said Kyra.

"Sounds like a big night, I have to choose my outfit," Lang said.

"Just make sure you do not wear your best stockings," Kyra said laughing out loud.

"Sister, I am wearing white knee high socks with my black low heel shoes."

Lang pulled out a black skirt and red blouse, "This is what I will be wearing sister."

"Yes, because red is your favorite color, and you look beautiful in red," said Kyra.

"Just as I love to see you Kyra in any shade of blue. Both of us have a different style but with elegance. I am not sure if I want a date on Saturday night," replied Lang.

"Well, our two friends from the fair will be there I am sure. I have enjoyed our times together but that's about all, no real connection for me Lang." replied Kyra.

"I feel the same Kyra, so how will we get to Wall Street," replied Lang.

"Ask Papa to drop us off and we will get the young men to bring us back. I do not want him to come back and get us, because it will be later on Friday night."

"Kyra, I got this, big sister will take care of our ride."

"I know you will but with who? I am not riding with anyone that I do not know and who has been drinking."

"Kyra, by the time we leave, everybody will be sober, even me, haha."

"Lang, are you going to have your picture taken tonight? I need your red lipstick."

"Yes, I am. Are you ready? Tell Papa we are ready to go"

"Ladies enjoy, and do not be fast and drinking." Kyra, looked over at Lang.

"Yes sir," closing the car door.

"Lang, I want to get my picture taken early because I do not want my hair looking crazy. Look, the booth is open already." The girls walked over to the booth.

"We want one picture together and one alone."

The photographer said, "You are two beautiful ladies."

"Thanks." They both smiled walking away, saying, "We will be back later for the pictures."

The band was playing Happy Birthday Bubba, and everybody was partying. Bubba, the birthday guy, came over to Kyra and said, "May I have this dance?" Kyra nodded her head and they went out to the dance floor and began dancing. After their dance, Lang walks up to Kyra.

"Kyra, I have our ride home, you ready? The club is closing in 30 minutes," Lang whispered in Kyra's ear.

"Bubba, I have to leave. My sister is ready, goodnight," said Kyra, as she was sitting with Bubba talking after their dance.

"I have our pictures," said Lang as they were leaving the club. They arrived back home and showed their mom the pictures they took.

Philantha said, "I will buy frames for them the next time I go to town. Kyra, you had the dreamy eye and serious look with your head tilted."

"I love my outfit Mom, I felt so special."

"Lang, you looked so elegant in that red blouse with the red lips."

"Thanks Mom."

"You look like you are in a deep thought," Philantha said to Lang.

"I am," replied Lang. "Can we talk?"

"Okay."

"I will go check on the girls," said Kyra as she walked out of the room.

"I would love for you to live here forever Lang, but this is your life and if you think this will help you and the girls I will support you. You have grown up so fast with two children, experiencing heart aches that has brought you pain. Polly and Ammy are so young they will be just fine here with us. You have to work and pay rent that would be a bit much without the fathers helping you in the city."

"I want so much more for the girls than what I have accomplished," replied Lang.

"You have been a great Mom and I love you Lang. You will see that there are more opportunities waiting for you, girl. I will speak to Tilton."

"Thanks Mom, I love you."

*****

The next day, Philantha was cooking the fish that Rider and Boe caught the day before.

"Smelling good Mom, are you cooking cornbread?" asked Kyra.

"Yes, Kyra can you set the table and call the family to wash up for dinner?" said Philantha.

Papa was checking on the cow which was grazing in the grass. Rider ran out to get him and they walked back together.

"Papa, Bessie is getting fat; she is due in a few days. Can I watch the birth?"

"You can help Rider, I know you are young Rider, but I do you think you will be a farmer."

"Papa I will take the knowledge that you have given me daily which can be helpful in any area of my life but I know I am not a farmer."

"Times are changing. Rider."

"I understand, Papa."

"Whatever you choose to pursue, never forget your roots. Some generations work harder than the next, so always build on where you came from, and never look down on anyone. Heritage is important, so imagine at your young age what you'll leave for the next generation." Rider was listening as Papa continued to teach him about life.

"Will you bring increase, or will you cause someone in your family to wonder what Rider accomplished? Remember all of us cannot be the greatest to the world, but we can all be the greatest to our family in one way or another. We are not our own because we live for more than just me, myself, and I."

"Papa, you are a man of wisdom, a hard worker and you desire positive growth for your family." They arrived back at the house.

Boe said, "Rider, what took you so long to find Papa?"

"Papa and I had a great conversation, so I was walking slowly to digest all that Papa was telling me."

Papa walked up and said, "Boe, I was telling Rider the importance of heritage."

Later that night Kyra and Lang were talking in their room.

"Kyra, will you ride the bus and bring the girls to see me when I move?" said Lang.

"I have never ridden a bus, but I will think about it, it will be less of a hassle for you to come to us," said Kyra.

Lang replied, "Brother said we will be visiting together when I move with him, that's a done deal, I will have to push him because he is so busy with a new position on his job.'"

"What type of job will you apply for?"

"A waitress, brother works in a restaurant that has an opening for waitresses every six months. So I will apply and pray that they hire me for the job. I have the experience; Mom has taught us well in serving others. Brother has favor with the manager and he is sure that once they know I am his sister I am hired."

"Yes, that will be favor Lang."

"Until that time comes, we have so much to share and accomplish as young ladies with Mom and my girls. Polly and Ammy are so young. Polly loves being in the kitchen with Mom because she allows her to mix the dry ingredients when she is cooking. Polly will be cooking earlier than you or I. Ammy loves to hang out more with Boe and his books, while Rider loves swimming and throwing balls."

"Lang, have you taken notice at how Ammy watches me every time I give you a hair style and wants to help. Polly is like forget the hair, I am going to help Grandmom shell the butter beans while you all look in the mirror and pamper yourself."

## Chapter 6

# Understanding Life

Philantha was in the bedroom folding clothes. She called out to the girls, "Come with me outside and help me bring all the clothes off the clothesline, the sky was getting darker and darker, the wind was starting to blow."

"Mom those clouds are mighty dark, that is a sign of wind and rain, watch the animals in the yard, I believe they have a sense that tells them to run for cover." All the chickens had gone in the hen house and the dogs that were home were on the back porch, not in the yard.

"Lang, go close the hen house door, Rider check on the calf; Tilton has the cow." Boe put the mules in the stable and shut the doors. I have a feeling we will have some strong winds with this rain. Where is Old Yeller?"

"He is with your Papa in the field," said Philantha. Kyra was bringing the clothes in the house with her mom. Ammy and Polly were on the back porch looking and waiting for everybody to come in the house.

Rider called out to Papa and replied, "I do not see him Mom." The winds were strong now and the rain was pouring.

"Everybody in the house, he should be here soon." Suddenly, the porch door blew off the hinges.

"What was that Mom?"

"Everybody let's go in the family room." Ammy and Polly were scared of the loud noise from the winds.

"God, we thank you for covering Tilton and us and our neighbors. Listen Lang, it sounds like a train passing by the house," said Philantha. There were cracking sounds and then a boom, the house shook.

"That had to be a tree that just fell," said Boe.

"Rider, get over here." He was looking out the window.

"The glass from the window could blow out in your face, boy."

"Mom, the big tree in the front yard is gone." The noise subsided but the rain was still pouring.

"It sounds like the worst is over," said Philantha.

Ammy and Polly said, "Not until we see Papa. Then I will not be afraid." A few moments later, Tilton walks up on the back porch and the dogs start barking and jumping. They were glad to see him too, Old Yeller was under the house. He saw that the back door was gone.

"Papa, where were you?"

"Kids, give him space to sit down and take off the wet boots and clothes then he can tell us the story."

"We were so scared," said Polly.

Tilton replied, "I was concerned about you all but I had to find a safe place from the strong winds. I tied Anna to a tree, and I jumped in the nearest ditch and covered my eyes and prayed."

"Philantha, that was the strongest tornadoes winds I have ever witnessed. We have plenty of wood for the heater this winter from the big tree that fell in the front yard. I am so thankful that no one was hurt," said Tilton.

"Lang, it is times like this that you realize the importance of family love," said Kyra.

"That is the truth, Kyra. I will never forget this experience with you all," said Tilton. The next day families on both sides of the road were cleaning up the yards, and fixing windows. Tilton was building a new door for the back porch. The sun was shining brighter than ever, the calm after the storm. The water in the well was so high you could almost dip the water from the well with the dipper.

"Quilting day will be moved to next week because of everybody cleaning up from the winds," said Philantha.

"The wedding is soon Philantha, my friend was talking about his daughter preparing to have a dinner and inviting the neighbors," said Tilton.

"Yes Tilton, everybody will bring a dish, so we will have plenty of food," said Philantha.

"What will you make Philantha?"

"Three large barbecue chickens and pies. We will be outside in their back yard. There will be food, fun, music and friends. The young man that is getting married lives near town. I met him last week; he is a tall statue of a man with a big infectious laugh."

"The pants that I am wearing to dinner, are a little longer than I like with the shoes. Can you hem them Philantha?" asked Tilton.

"Put them on now Tilton, so I can mark them for later." Tilton passed Polly standing by the window daydreaming with tears in her eyes.

"Polly why are you crying?"

"Papa, I do not want my mom to leave. I prayed that she would stay."

"God will give you peace Polly, so that you will someday understand that in life we do not always get exactly what we want, but it may be what we need. As the old song goes, *You Will Understand It By and By*."

"What does that mean Papa?"

"As you live your life you will see why your mother moved away and you and Ammy stayed here with us. It is your mom's desire to move, and find herself, so pray for her peace. She loves you both very much."

"Mom is a lot like you Papa, I love you both." Polly hugged him tight and ran to find Ammy and Rider. In the other room, Lang went to go find Kyra so that she could ask for help with her hair.

"Kyra, come help me with a new hair style," said Lang.

"Lang, we need to learn how to finger wave our own hair," said Kyra.

"When I am in town this week," replied Lang.

"Oh no, this is my week to go with Papa," said Kyra.

"We both can go if Mom is not going. I will buy some hair spray along with the royal crown. For the marriage dinner, I will get Cousin Bee to finger wave my hair. She does a great job," said Lang.

"Yes she does, replied Kyra.

Lang said, "With the coarseness of our hair, we may need two jars of grease" They both laughed and laughed.

"Sister we have to look our best at the dinner, who knows, we may meet our husbands," said Kyra.

"I desire a city boy myself," said Lang.

"That's your desire. My desire is a man with a slow hand, city or country," said Kyra as she laughed.

"You are nasty Kyra."

"What?"

"Girl do you know what a slow hand man is? A slow hand man is one that will not be in a hurry or rush with whatever he does for me and with me, always willing to satisfy his lady," said Lang.

"Now am I so nasty?" replied Kyra.

"Sounds like you know exactly what you want in a man," said Lang.

"Kyra! Are you ready, our ride is waiting." It was Bubba and a friend that wanted to meet Lang.

"This maybe my last time with you for a while on Wall Street. I heard back from brother, he wants me to come out in three weeks and apply for the job as a waitress."

"We can talk about this later. Let's go have fun together."

"Kyra are you ignoring me?" asked Lang.

"I do not want to think about you not being here with me, who will I talk to at night in bed until I fall asleep in the dark quiet room?" asked Kyra.

The music was playing loud. "Look Lang, that is the young girl who will be getting married that Mom and the ladies have been quilting together over the past months," said Kyra.

"Is that her husband to be with her," asked Lang.

"No, I think that is one of her brothers, she has five brothers," said Kyra.

"How do you know?" asked Lang.

"Papa told me he is friends with their father. The young man that I asked about at the club months ago is one of her brothers, Boone is his name," replied Kyra.

"Now I see, that is the one I called the dancer with her."

"Let us go sit with our dates, before they leave us here to walk home," said Kyra.

"Kyra we will never have any problems getting a ride home."

"I know that is right sister."

# Chapter 7

# Lang Plans to Move Away

Wall Street was crowded. "Why so many extra people tonight?" asked Lang.

"Boone's sister's husband to be is celebrating with a lot of his friends. He is a well known young man. Lang, look over to your right at three o'clock that is Boone."

"Wow! I see what you mean sister, if he does not have a slow hand give him to me. Just kidding he is not my city man," said Lang.

They both ran out on the floor and started dancing. "Bubba asked me if we could be closer than friends. I am not attracted to him. Bubba is very kind, handsome, and a gentleman," said Kyra.

"What is it about him you do not like?" asked Lang.

"I am not sure, but my heart does not skip a beat when he touches me or even calls my name," replied Kyra.

"Is his hand slow?" asked Lang jokingly.

"Stop Lang."

"What Kyra? I am sure you will know without a doubt when the right one comes your way." They finish their conversation and Bubba walks over.

"Kyra, can I have this dance?" asked Bubba. As they were dancing close Bubba said, "Kyra you are a beautiful lady."

"And you Bubba, are a gentleman, I have enjoyed my night with you."

*****

The next morning, the Kyra and Lang walked into the kitchen. "Girls you both came in late last night, said Philantha." They were moving very slow.

"Yes Mom, it was a fun night with so many people. It was like a holiday gathering."

"Come help me finish breakfast, today is quilting day at Bee's house. So, I will be across the road for a few hours. We will be finishing today. Tilton will be back from feeding the animals soon," said Philantha.

"Did he have coffee Mom?"

"Yes, the coffee pot is still on the stove because he will want more with his breakfast."

Polly walked in rubbing her eyes and yawning. "Ammy always gets up so early and wake me to playhouse with her" said Polly.

Ammy ran into the room smiling. "I am so hungry, Mom."

"I hear Tilton on the back porch washing up with Rider and Boe. Let's all sit down to eat," said Philantha.

"Philantha, I have a hog that I am fattening to be killed in a few weeks."

"Sounds good Papa, I love barbecue," said Rider.

Boe spoke up and said, "Kyra, I know you love the sausage more, so you can eat with Mom's biscuits. I love every way Mom cooks the hog."

"Sorry Rider I will not be barbecuing this one. We will have ham, sausage, fatback, and chitterlings," said Philantha.

Polly said, "I just do not like chitterlings. They are so nasty, right Ammy?"

"I agree with Boe." They all laughed as they finished eating.

"Seven thirty, I have to get ready to leave, clean up ladies."

Tilton, Rider and Boe were going fishing.

"Lang, what are your plans for today?" asked Kyra.

"I have to prepare myself and the girls for my move so we are spending time doing anything they want to do today," said Lang.

"Well, I guess I will go practice the finger waves," said Kyra.

"No, come with us first."

"Where are you going?" asked Kyra.

"They want to surprise Papa at the creek and they really want to swim," said Lang.

"They cannot swim, and fish in the same creek, it will scare the fish away," said Kyra.

"Polly and Ammy, that is the truth, so we will have to go next week. You know tomorrow is Sunday, and hair day is this evening," replied Lang.

"Mom can we just go outside in the front yard under the umbrella tree and you read a book or two?"

"Lang I will go out front with you all because you know I was not getting my hair wet today," replied Kyra.

"Okay Kyra, you read one story, I will read one and then we can talk about the move," said Lang.

*****

Cousin Bee welcomed everybody to the quilting gathering. "Ladies so glad to see you all and thank God for taking care of each one of us last week during those damaging winds. We have come to finish this beautiful quilt, and catch up on each other's lives. Philantha you seem to be distant this morning what is so heavy on your mind?"

"My oldest daughter Lang, has plans to move away from home soon and the two grands will be staying with me," said Philantha.

"How far?" Asked one of the ladies.

"Up north to the city. So many young people want to move up north now, wanting more than the country life more opportunities. Each generation should want more than the previous. I do want more for my children, but I will miss her and the girls too, enough about me ladies," said Philantha.

"The bride will love this quilt on those cold nights with her husband. We pray a long union with lots of kids to fill their home with lots of love and noise. Thanks lady, I enjoyed our time together, see you all soon," said Cousin Bee.

Polly and Ammy ran down the dirt path to meet Philantha. "Hey girls."

"We missed you Grandmom."

"Missed you too." She sat in one of the chairs under the umbrella tree. Lang was answering a question from Polly when the kids ran to meet Philantha. Polly asked, "What is a waitress? I wait our table for Grandmom, so am I a waitress?"

"Yes, you are with less responsibility. Your mom will have to take the people's food orders and then go to the kitchen, get the food and carry on a good conversation, so she will get a good tip."

"Mom will get great tips because she is not afraid to talk to anybody," said Polly.

"Mom you can send me the money and I can buy more dolls and tea sets to play house with Polly. I want money to give Grandmom money to buy all the fabric to make lots of dresses and skirts for me for school," said Ammy.

"Sounds great girls."

"I will see that you both get what you want." Kyra was looking for four leaf clovers in the cluff of clovers under the umbrella tree.

"Here Lang, I found one for you."

"Thanks, sister I want all the good luck in the world for you," said Kyra.

"No matter what comes my way, I know I have all I need with my family. Whatever I learn and experience in this life will be a plus. You all know that is one of the meanings of Tilton's name, Clover. Clovers have no wood stems, which come from the pea family."

"So, if Papa is the big clover, that makes us the small cuffs of clovers in his life mom."

" Yes" Kyra.

Polly said, "Grandmom I want to be a four-leaf clover myself."

"Ammy, you can be a three." Ammy smiled as she played with her doll on the grass.

"Polly, clovers come in many types, the one you are looking at now is from the white clover family which is called four leaf clovers, and the common leaf is three leaf. The traditions of folk before my time gave meaning to each leaf. The first leaf is for hope, the second leaf is faith, the third leaf love and the fourth leaf luck to the finder. The fifth leaf is money and some even say, if you ever come across a sixth leaf, it is fame and the seventh leaf longevity. Do you only want the four leaf now?"

"Well, it sounds like any one is good, but the fifth is money. So I will be looking for the fifth leaf everywhere I see the cuffs of clovers."

Tilton and the boys came from around the back with two strings of fish. "You all ready for some fish for dinner?" Everybody was smiling and said out loud, "Yes!"

Rider looked at Kyra and said, "I caught this big one for you because I know how much you love fish sister."

"Thanks Rider," said Kyra. They all walked to the back yard together. Tilton placed the fish on the shelf he made on the back porch to cut meat, clean fish, and chitterlings, so that he would not mess up Philantha's kitchen. Boe goes to get the firewood as Tilton cleaned the fish. Lang left to get the grease to melt in the big black pot. The pot is hot ready for the grease. Kyra went in the house to get the salt and corn meal for the fish. Philantha was mixing corn meal for cornbread and warming soup for the side.

"Smells good in here Mom, today has been a family day of fun for us all," said Kyra.

## Chapter 8
# Kyra Meets the Love of Her Life

"Kyra, supper tonight will be whatever is left from dinner because we have to cook for tomorrow and Sunday dinner. Tilton's sister and her family will be eating with us tomorrow."

Boe said, "Papa, I like her oldest son, we talk about the books we read and share our thoughts."

"Cousins are like your distant sisters and brothers Boe."

"Lang, Mom read Psalm 23, to us yesterday and then it was the lesson for Sunday school. I remember it in the prayer as we ate dinner yesterday, mom how did you know?"

"The booklet for Sunday school, I had studied it already, and I just prepared you all beforehand. Kyra so as we memorize Psalm 23, we will read it out loud so that Polly and Ammy can listen."

"Welcome family, wash your hands, supper is ready." Tilton was hugging his sister.

Ammy said, "Papa, she looks just like you."

"This is my sister give her a hug," said Tilton.

"No problem." They hugged and Ammy whispered in her ear, "Are you quiet like my Papa?" She smiled rubbing Ammy's head.

Boe made sure he sat with his cousin. They talked about comic books. "What are you reading?" asked Boe.

"I just started my comic book *Detective Dan*," replied Harry.

"Great I am reading *Tip Top Comics*, my next visit to the five and dime store I will purchase the funny for the family comic book. I was looking at popular comic books the last time I was there. I think I will purchase that one next, there are so many great comic books," replied Boe.

Rider listened as the boys talked and then said, "I want to learn how to read books, Boe read me a scary story last week, but I was dreaming about the killer all night. My favorite one is Mickey Mouse and Tarzan stories."

"All are great to read to me, I love a variety of books," said Harry.

"Harry, you are a great reader, maybe you will be a schoolteacher."

After supper, while Kyra and Lang were cleaning up the kitchen, Lang wanted to have an important talk with her about dating. "Kyra, I want to talk to you about protection when you become sexually active. We make mistakes sometimes and we have to try to help someone else avoid the ones we made, if they will listen and apply what is being said. I got pregnant twice being careless and not being accountable for my actions and allowed the young men not to be responsible. Do not allow young men to tell you no when you ask them to use protection. Know yourself that you need to be protected from any disease and pregnancy. The best protection is to abstain until you are married with someone that you love and want to raise children with."

"Lang, I love you, you may have made two wrong decisions, but your girls are not mistakes. Polly and Ammy are two gifts from God that were meant to be here with us all."

Lang gave Kyra a big hug, "I love you too."

*****

The next day the family is getting ready to attend a wedding dinner. Lang was doing Ammy's hair.

"Ammy, please sit still I have to finish your hair so I can get dressed."

"But Mom, my doll will not sit still, so she is making me move my head."

"Girl, you always have an answer when you want to do what you want too, just listen," said Lang.

"Sorry Mom, I will."

"Polly, you look pretty. Fix the ruffle on your socks and turn them down, we are almost ready to leave."

"Can I ride on the back of the truck with Rider and Boe?" asked Ammy.

"I will have to ride with you Ammy, so you can sit between my legs because you cannot ride on the tail gate with Rider and Boe on the very end of the truck, that is scary to me."

"Papa let me ride to the barn on the back, and I sat between Boe's legs as he held my top so I would not fall."

"That was because he was driving slow and not on the road."

"Papa always drives slow Mom."

"Well, he was going extra slow and there were no other cars near you."

"I will ride on the back and we will sit at the back of the cab of the truck and not sit on the tail gate. We only have five miles to go up the road."

Tilton placed the food on the back of the truck. "Please do not allow the pans to move around and spill over girls."

"I got this Papa." Kyra ran out of the house.

"Aunt Kyra come ride on the back with us."

"I am riding in the front so that my hair stays in place," replied Kyra.

"You have on a scarf girl," said Lang.

"I know. I will take the scarf off when I get there because I do not want to sweat out my finger waves, plus the scarf keeps them in place."

"Lang, look there is Boone, and he does not have a girl with him nor his brothers. They look handsome in their button down white shirts."

The bride and groom stood up and thanked everybody for coming to celebrate their union.

"Wow! He is tall, and she is so short. Her mom is short and so cute sitting beside them on the right with her handsome husband. That's where the boys got their good looks from their father." Everyone was eating and talking enjoying each other. The bride and groom thanked everyone again for all the gifts and especially the neighborhood quilt made with the many colors to represent many children and all the prayers of blessings of their union.

"Lang, I have to meet Boone today," said Kyra.

"Okay, we will make this happen Kyra." Meanwhile, Rider was playing with his truck with soldiers on the back. Boone approached Rider.

"Hello little man, what is your name?"

"I am Rider. What's your name?"

"Boone."

"Okay, you want to play with my soldiers?"

"No, I just wanted to see your soldiers. You have Army and Navy soldiers?" asked Boone.

"Yes, my Army soldiers are taking my navy soldier to his boat."

"How do you know so much about the soldiers?"

"My brother, Boe reads all types of books and he reads them to me. Sometimes he reads scary stories. Do you like to read? I will be glad when I can read all by myself," replied Rider.

"You are very direct Rider, to be so young."

"I am almost four and my birthday is soon, my sister Kyra's on the same day."

"Wow! Cool."

"Come see my sister." He took Boone by the hand and pulled him toward Kyra.

"Okay slow up." Rider was almost running.

"Lang, Rider and Boone are talking as they walk towards us," said Kyra.

35

"Keep calm this is your chance," said Lang. Rider was still holding Boone's hand.

"Hello ladies, my name is Boone."

"Hello, my name is Lang, and my name is Kyra." Both the girls were smiling. "It is a pleasure to meet you both," replied Boone.

Rider said," Bye," as he ran off to play.

"So, Kyra you are the one with the same birthday as Rider," said Boone.

"Yes, I always tell people God gave him to me as my birthday present, and he is my baby. If he gets in trouble, I cannot go out and I have to stay home to keep him." They laughed together and talked the whole day. Kyra jumped on the back of the truck to ride home.

"What about your hair Auntie Kyra?"

"What hair? I just want to ride with the breeze in my face to wake me up. I have just met Boone. Thank you Rider, you were born for this day."

"What day Kyra?"

"To introduce me to Boone. When I go to town next week, I will be sure to get you some candy and some cookies." Boe looked at Rider.

"You have favor with people as a young boy."

"Boys bring all the pans off the truck to the kitchen so the girls can clean them."

"The food was so good Mom."

"Thanks, it really was a great gathering, and the bride loved the quilt from the community." Lang could not get a word in for Kyra's excitement of the day.

"Okay Lang, I will calm myself for a little while. I saw you talking to Boone's brother, the dancer," said Kyra.

"Yes, we had great conversation; he seemed to be a nice young man. Miles said that he and Boone talked about seeing us at the club several times. He asked if we could double date one night, maybe go to Wall Street. He mentioned that neither one of them are in serious relationships at the moment and smiled. They are less than two years a part, but Boone is the oldest," said Lang.

"Boone did tell me he was thinking about going to the Navy to get away from home. Military does give you great opportunities to meet others and experience different parts of the world. The war is the worst part because so many lose their lives and mental stability. Our brothers just enlisted, they are so young to fight for our country. The sign showed Uncle Sam always pointing to a few good men, so they volunteer to serve their country. Maybe they can avoid another war while they are serving," repled Kyra.

## Chapter 9

# Brother Drives Lang to the City

"Kyra, I will get my ticket one day this week from the bus station in town. Brother told me; I have to come earlier than planned because the restaurant needs workers."

"Lang, you leaving and I just met Boone," said Kyra. Kyra was sad for days. Polly and Ammy were playing outside on the porch. Tilton was inside listening to the radio, and Philantha was folding clothes. Kyra looked out the window down the path of beautiful flowers and she saw an unknown car driving up the path. The girls called out, "Here comes a car." It was a shiny green car with a glass roof top, and the driver was smiling. Brother opened the door and everybody was so glad to see him. They all gave him a hug.

"Hello son, I am surprised to see you, nice car," said Tilton.

"Thanks Papa, I decided to come pick Lang up so she would not have to ride the bus." Philantha was waiting to get her hug.

"Hey Mom."

"Hey son, miss you, how are you?"

"I am good, I had a good trip."

"Will you stay overnight?" asked Philantha.

"Yes, I told Lang I would give her a few more days so I can play with Polly and Ammy." The girls smiled.

"I know you are hungry let's go to the kitchen." They walk into the kitchen and Lang explained brother's surprise arrival.

"The last letter he wrote, he told me he was trying to come, but was not sure if he would get the time off work. I did not want to tell you Kyra, we could never have enough time together," said Lang. They were both crying and holding hands.

"I miss you already," said Kyra.

"Mom, I will just eat some soup, I am not very hungry. I will wait to get a big meal with you all for supper," said Lang.

"Ok, I will warm some soup and I have some biscuits from breakfast, sounds good." Papa and brother walked outside in the back yard to talk alone.

"You are still so young, enjoy your life before you commit to anyone else. It is not easy taking care of a family son."

"My plans are to wait. I like my job and I do have some great friends. Papa, sometimes my anger still rules, I was in a fight last week after a young man hit his lady and I got involved."

"I know you would not stand for that, but please be careful okay."

"How are you Papa?"

"Just thinking of Lang leaving and not knowing how Polly and Ammy will adjust to the change," said Tilton.

"I will make sure I bring Lang home to see them when I can get off work."

Tilton replied, "Kyra is here to help. Sometimes they obey Kyra better than Lang. Kyra seems to be born to be a mother, and will be a great one when she has her own. I pray it will not be anytime soon."

*****

Lang ran to the car and laid her head back on the neck rest and cried so the girls would not see her, they all waved goodbye while crying. Kyra would not come out of her room.

"Polly can you play with me since Mom is not here to drink the tea with me and my doll Becky?"

"Sure Ammy."

"Mom said she will write us every week and visit very soon." Kyra was thinking about Lang, the girls, and the date they never had with Boone and his brother. For days Kyra was so quiet she barely talked to the girls. Rider wanted to cheer her up.

"Aunt Kyra, uncle brought me some men to play with. Can you tell me what this man does with a gun like Papa's?"

"You have different men in the military. They are called soldiers."

"Yes, that is what uncle told me."

"Some learn to fly airplanes, some serve on boats, and some have to walk the ground. You will understand better when you are older, so it is nothing you have to think about at your age little man. Now you can pretend to be fighting."

"This one looks like Popeye."

"Popeye is in the Navy, he rides on the boat. And the green ones are like my older uncles in the Army. I will let all my men ride in my truck so they can fight the bad men together."

"Rider, always pray for the soldiers when you say your prayers at night," said Kyra.

"Lord give protection to our soldiers and Lang, right?" asked Rider.

"Yes, good Rider."

"I miss Lang," Rider quietly added.

"Me too Rider. When I write her, I will tell her you said hello okay, and tell her to come home too."

"Kyra, can we go to the mailbox? I saw the mail man pass by the path, I was looking out the window. Ammy, come walk to the mailbox with us."

"Girls, maybe tomorrow you will have a letter from your mom," said Kyra.

"Tomorrow can you wait until the girls are awake to come to the barn? I want to go early with the other ladies," said Philantha.

*****

The community always came together when it was tobacco season to help each other on different days of the week.

"Who will hand tobacco to you until I get there?"

"Cousin Bee will be with me and her daughter Lizzie."

"Polly wake up, Ammy go back to sleep."

"I cannot sleep Becky was scared and I am hungry. Hold my hand, I am still hungry okay."

"You girls are up early, Polly."

"Yes Ammy, could not sleep; now we can all go to the barn together Kyra." Rider is taking the plate of scraps to the dogs. Boe is with Tilton in the tobacco field; they will be at the barn soon with a trailer of tobacco ready to be tied on the sticks.

# Chapter 10

# Kyra's Attraction for Boone

Everybody was at Cousin Bee's and ready to work bright and early in the morning. "Good morning family, Philantha have you heard from the newlyweds? It has been four months," said Cousin Bee.

"Girl, the quilt prayer is working already really; she is one month with child. In the bible in Psalm 127:5 it says happy is the man, who has his quiver full of them quiver quilt."

They both laughed out loud then Kyra said, "Girl I love it when we are together."

"I know how you must be missing Lang" said Aunt Bee.

"Yes, staying busy with Polly and Ammy makes the changes easier."

"Kyra, you need to spend more time with Lizzie, you are just a year younger than her."

"Sounds like a plan to me," replied Kyra.

"Right mom," Lizzie replied and then continued, "You know I have my license and my dad allows me to drive his car."

"Lizzie, I have never seen you on Wall Street at the club in town."

"My mom did not allow us to dance at home when I was younger, so I never had the desire, but I am old enough now. I spend a lot of time with my boyfriend, we are getting serious, so I need to go out more before he asks me to get married, and then I will be barefoot and pregnant."

"So, let's plan for this Friday night, if it is okay with your boyfriend. Just you and I, you can hook up after we get to the club, but we will leave together."

"Ammy, after dinner we will go to the mailbox." She ran to tell Polly.

"Polly! Aunt Kyra will take us to get the mail. Are you ready?"

"Yes," replied Ammy.

"Okay she is waiting on the porch, Rider wants to come." They all went together, walking slow and looking at the flowers. Rider was looking for a five-leaf clover.

"I found one! Look it is a four leaf."

"That is hard to find Rider, today is your lucky day."

"Right sister." Mr. mailman is just coming down the road, he stopped as they walked near the mailbox off the side of the road.

"Good afternoon, Kyra you have lots of mail today," he said as he handed Kyra the mail.

"Thank you, Sir." She took the letters and walked back to the children.

Rider ran ahead of them saying, "I know, I do not have any mail." The first letter was for Kyra.

"Aunt, is there one for us?" the girls asked.

"Not yet girls, looks like the other letter is for Mom and Papa." Polly and Ammy dropped their heads and then ran ahead of Kyra as she read her letter. Lang wrote:

> Kyra, life is good, but I miss you so much and the girls. I am working six days a week; I chose these days. I have one day to sleep, but once I rent my own apartment, I will not work as hard. I have to have my own space since the boys are so messy. I am living with brother and two friends. He is on the crouch and I have his room. There is nothing like living with you. I understand now what you were saying about keeping the room clean every day, and never skipping a day. Well, we missed a few days and I said to myself, I need Kyra in this house. I eat at the restaurant daily, so I have not been cooking. I think I lost a few pounds.

Kyra turned to the third page and there was a page to the girls and there was a check for Kyra. She called to the girls, "Polly and Ammy, come here, I have something for you."

"What Aunt Kyra?" they asked.

"A letter from your mom," Kyra replied. The girls were jumping up and down and laughing so much Philantha came to the door.

"You all okay?"

"Yes Mom, they have a letter from Lang. Here Mom, these are for you and Papa," Kyra told her as she handed her the letters.

"Thanks," said Philantha. Lang had written to the whole family that day and sent money home to take care of the girls. Tilton and Philantha were glad to have extra money.

"Thanks Aunt Kyra for reading the letter to us," said the girls.

"I feel better too because she said hi to me," said Rider.

Boe said, "I am too, and we can go to town and get the comic books this week with the money she sent to Aunt Kyra to give you and I, a dollar. I have never had that much money at one time."

"Put some in your piggy bank she said in the letter," replied Kyra.
"I plan to only spend fifty cents and save fifty."
"Rider, mom will keep yours," said Kyra.
"I just want cookies because Boe, will read to me from his books."
"I may have to charge you Rider," said Boe laughing.

*****

There will be a neighborhood barn yard gathering this weekend with food, music, and hayrides.

"Kyra, have you made plans for Saturday afternoon between three and nine? Philantha and I will attend the barnyard affair with the family," said Tilton.

"I will make plans to be there Papa, with Lizzie and her boyfriend.

Lizzie was blowing her horn, "Kyra, your ride is outside,"

"Thanks Mom see you all later" Kyra replied as she left the house and opened the door to the car.

"Hi Lizzie."

"Hi Kyra," Lizzie responded as she started driving.

"What did your boyfriend say about us going out together?" asked Kyra.

"He was good. He had plans for tonight himself. We decided to give each other more time with other people, I love him, and we trust each other."

"You both are still young."

Lizzie said, "We need to find a park on this side of the street where we will be close to the building."

Kyra and Lizzie spotted a few young ladies sitting up front near the band, where the DJ played.

"Hello ladies, may we sit with you all tonight?" they asked.

"Sure we would love to have your company." One of the ladies stood up and said, "Let's go get some drinks."

Lizzie leaned over to Kyra and said, "I do not drink beer when I am driving."

"Good, because my brothers have scared me riding with them from the club drinking and talking loud," Kyra replied.

"Let's get a root beer float"

"Sounds good." The tables were full now in the club, the music began, and Kyra was one of the first ones on the floor hand dancing with one of the ladies from her group. When the next song played, Kyra asked Lizzie to dance.

"I will lead."

"Kyra you are a great dancer and teacher, I am really enjoying myself," Lizzie said as they walked back to their seat.

The DJ introduced the band, which Bubba played the guitar. The lead lady was singing Billy Holiday's song, "The Man I Love." Kyra felt a tap on her shoulder, as she looked up, it was Boone.

"May I have this dance?" Boone asked as he walked up to Kyra. She froze. "Kyra, you okay? You look like you saw a ghost," Boone said as he extended his hand.

"Hello Boone, I would love to dance," she said. Kyra smiled as she took his hand. This was a slow song, so they were close enough to talk. His mouth was close to Kyra's ear.

"Good to see you here alone Kyra."

She pulled back "How did you know I was alone?" she asked.

"I saw you when you and your girl came in the club," he said. Kyra leaned back with her head near his face and all she could think of was how gentle he was with his hands, Kyra smiled on the inside, and her heart was skipping with joy.

"Are you alone Boone?" There was a pause,

"I am with my brother tonight," said Boone.

"You know what I meant," they both laughed out loud. Boone walked Kyra back to her seat.

"Kyra who was that gentlemen?" asked Lizzie.

She was still smiling, and her mind was still on the dance floor, dazed with his smell thinking she would never forget the smooth thick rich smell of Boone's neck.

"I am sorry Lizzie; I have such a strong attraction to this young man. I have spoken with him maybe three times and tonight he asked me to dance. I feel like, well I really cannot explain my feelings" Kyra explained. Then Bubba walked up to Kyra's table.

"Hello Kyra. How are you ladies?"

"Hello, Bubba, I saw you on the dance floor, so I came over to speak. May we talk alone?"

"Yes," Kyra said, "Lizzie, I will be back in a few moments?"

"Kyra you never gave me an answer about dating," said Bubba "I like you a lot."

"But I am not ready for a serious relationship," replied Kyra.

"Sorry, that does not change the way I feel about you Kyra. I signed up for the Navy, so can we plan a date before I leave?"

"Sure Bubba," Kyra said.

"I have two months before I leave."

They said their goodbye's and then Kyra went to go find Lizzie. She found Lizzie and they left Wall Street together.

Kyra said, "Lizzie tonight was a very interesting night. There is one man who cares for me, but I am not wild over him at all and, another man that causes a warm smooth flow of scents to my heart that only my heart can smell."

Lizzie said, "I have never had that feeling in my heart for my boyfriend."

"Lizzie, check your heart scents," Kyra told her.

"How can I check scents of my heart, Kyra?" asked Lizzie.

"The next time you come to my house in the daytime, I will teach you with my mother's flowers," Kyra said.

"How about tomorrow at the barnyard gathering? I cannot wait to get my lesson Kyra."

"Okay, Goodnight Lizzie," said Kyra as she closed the car door and walked up on the porch at her home.

The next day, the birds were chirping very loud at Kyra's window. Kyra was singing, "Sun in the sky, you know how I feel, it's a new life for me, and I am feeling good. Stars when you shine, you know how I feel, I am Feeling Good."

"Good morning Mom," Kyra said cheerfully.

"Sound like you had a great night sleep," Philantha replied.

"Yes Mom, my heart is happy."

"Kyra sometimes your heart will not be happy, but remember happiness is a choice when you surrender your feelings, or know what you want in life. Life is full of ups and downs. Enjoy your happiness Kyra."

"Mom are you happy?" Kyra asked.

"You being happy is what makes me happy Kyra." Lizzie walked up on the front porch where Philantha was seated in the rocking chair, Ammy and Polly were playing with the tea set.

"You are out early today. Go on in the house, Kyra is in her room."

"Hi Kyra, I came for my heart scent lesson," said Lizzie.

"Girl you are serious," said Kyra as they both walked out in the front yard.

"Lizzie, pull up one of those weeds, smell the weed, how does that scent affect your mood?" Kyra asked as Lizzie smelled the weed.

"It stinks so I will just throw it away."

"Let us try another type. Pull up one of those clovers and smell the clover," Kyra instructed.

"Not much smell to the clover, but I could keep the clover because it does not stink."

"Lizzie, keep the clover in your hand as we walk to the path of my mom's flowers. I want you to choose one of the flowers that you like the most," said Kyra.

"They all are beautiful Kyra," said Lizzie.

"But which one is for you," asked Kyra. Lizzie picked a purple one, Kyra picked a blue one.

"Lizzie, I want you to smell your flower as I smell mine." Lizzie closed her eyes to the smell.

"What did you feel?" Lizzie said,

"Mine told my heart to relax and enjoy the moment, so I closed my eyes and enjoyed the smell. As the scent flowed through my mind to my heart, that caused my heart to relax."

"Now smell the clover again Lizzie, what happens this time?"

"I fell different toward the clover the second time. Why?"

"Because of the awareness of relaxation and peace that the purple flower brought to my being. The clover did not add anything to my being, it was just a clover to me."

"So, if this were three young men, which would be your choice?" Kyra asked.

"That's easy Kyra, the purple man," Lizzie said.

"So do not settle for the stinky weed, or the bland clover. You can relate this to their attitude, their gentleness, their respect toward you, and the smell that arouse your senses. The heart scent test is complete. See you soon Lizzie."

"Okay around 4:00," Lizzie said as she left.

## Chapter 11

# Kyra and Boone's First Kiss

"Kyra, you and Lizzie are becoming close friends as well as cousins," Philantha said as she sat down in the kitchen.

"Mom we enjoy each other a lot."

"Girls, we will write to Lang tomorrow after church and mail the letter on Monday," said Philantha.

"I have a lot to share with her. I have a letter for Lang also to be mailed, but I need to get stamps from the mailman," said Kyra.

"Put a note with money for stamps in the mailbox on Monday because today is too late, it is after 12:00."

"Okay Mom, then we will have to mail the letter the next day." Kyra was getting ready to leave for the barnyard gathering.

Philantha asked, "Are you still coming with Lizzie?"

"Yes." Lizzie pulled up to the house and Kyra headed towards her.

"Lizzie, why are you so late?"

"My boyfriend got upset with me and would not let me come. I took into consideration the lesson I had today on the heart scent test. When he was talking to me, I heard disrespect like I had never heard before, and it was a stinky conversation. I told him I was not happy at the words he was saying to me. He said just go to the gathering without me, so I left and here I am, sorry I am late."

"Lizzie, please push past your pain and enjoy the gathering with me," Kyra said as she and Lizzie headed to the gathering. The music was playing, and people were eating and laughing.

"Kyra, a group of young men and women are going on a hayride at sunset. This will be the last one for today, let's join them."

"It sounds romantic Lizzie. Are you sure?"

"Yes, we will get to see the sunset and they have candy apples and peanuts for sale," Lizzie said as they boarded the wagon.

The driver said now there are eight young men and eight young women. But listen to this Kyra out of the 16 on board, 12 were couples, so that leaves two young ladies which are you and I and two young men."

"We do not have to couple up with anyone."

"Kyra I am ready to get me a good seat," said Lizzie. There was hay on the bottom of the wagon, and they placed stacks on top of the hay.

"I am glad I wore my blue trousers, so the hay will not scratch my legs."

"Lizzie, you should have brought your sweater you know we do not have anyone on here to keep you warm in the night air," said Kyra laughing so loud, that everybody on the ride looked back at her.

"Kyra!"

"Boone!" He got up and walked towards to the front of the wagon where Kyra and Lizzie were seated.

"Are you here alone?" Kyra asked.

"No Kyra, my brother is with me again. I see you are with your girl too," said Boone. The driver of the wagon said we are waiting on three people and we will be leaving.

"May I sit with you, Kyra?" asked Boone.

"Sure," replied Kyra.

"My brother will want to sit with us if that is okay with you." His brother walked to the back and sat on the same side as Lizzie.

"Hello, my name is Miles, and yours?"

"Lizzie nice to meet you," she replied.

"And good to see you again Kyra."

"Hello Miles," Kyra said. The tractor pulling the wagon began to move, the driver said all abroad. Boone had a bag of peanuts that he shared with Kyra. Miles had two apples and he gave one to Lizzie that he had brought for Boone. The trail was an hour ride, this was the driver's last trip for the day. He had to be close to the home when it got dark, because the tractor only had one large head light. Boone reached over and took Kyra's hand, she smiled.

"I am enjoying this time with you Kyra."

Miles was telling jokes and they all were laughing. Kyra was so into the joy in her heart she did not hear one joke. She laughed when everybody else laughed, but she could only hear the words that Boone was saying to her. They held hands for the last ten minutes of the ride, and then Boone pulled Kyra close to him and it was like she melted into his arms. Boone passionately kissed Kyra. Kyra's heart scents were running up and down her body like shock waves. Lizzie was enjoying Miles conversation so much that he asked if they could have a date, but Lizzie had to tell him the story of her boyfriend.

Kyra and Lizzie ride home was more interesting than before, this time it was Lizzie talking about how polite and respectful Miles was to her. He took her hand to help her from the wagon, and thanked her for allowing him to have a wonderful evening.

"Kyra, thanks again for the heart scent test," said Lizzie.

Kyra smiled all the way home, thinking of her kiss from Boone.

Kyra said, "Lizzie this has been a wonderful evening for us all." Lizzie dropped Kyra off at her house.

"Goodnight Kyra, see you soon." When Lizzie drove up to her house there was a car on the side of the path with its lights on. Lizzie recognized that the car was her boyfriend's. As Lizzie approached the car, she slowed down, rolled down the window and stopped her car. His window was already down.

"Hello Lizzie."

"Hello, why are you sitting here?"

"Waiting on you to come home from your date."

"I went on the hayride that you did not want to attend."

They had more words and Lizzie said, "I have to go in the house so, I will talk with you tomorrow."

Kyra woke up early the next morning because she had so much to write to Lang.

"Good morning Mom. If I wait for the mailman with the letter, do you think he will place the stamps on the letter?" Kyra asked.

Mom replied, "That is not his job, but he is generous, so just ask him."

"I already had three pages front to back that I wrote. I added another page this morning. Ammy and Polly had lots to say, so I will be sending two letters instead of one. Lang will be so happy to hear from us all."

## Chapter 12

# Life Changes Everyday

On Monday afternoon Kyra walked to the mailbox alone, while the girls were busy playing in mud. Kyra approached the mailbox as Lizzie's car was passing by, and she waved for Lizzie to stop. Lizzie stopped her car and Kyra walked toward her car as the mailman was pulling up to the box, "Wait Lizzie. Thanks Mr. mailman."

"You're welcome Kyra," he said then continued on his way.

"Hello Lizzie."

"Hello Kyra."

"Why are you speeding? Slow down."

Lizzie replied, "I did not realize I was speeding."

"Yes, just enough to get my attention," said Kyra.

Lizzie asked, "Can you ride with me?"

"Okay drive back up the path so I can tell Mom."

"Kyra, my thoughts are all over the place. I have to tell my boyfriend it is off for us, if he does not tell me first. It seems that he is trying to show me that its over in so many ways, but I am stuck on what really happened."

"People can grow apart in the midst of love, their desires change, and the communication changes. Change is a big part of all our lives."

"Thanks for riding with me to my cousins house, well, she is really our cousin." On the ride back they approached this tractor with three young men. They pulled over on the side of the road, waving them on, so Lizzie could drive pass them.

Kyra looked at the one driving and said, "That is Miles and Boone on the tractor Lizzie." Lizzie turned in to the next path and the tractor came behind them. They recognized the girls in the car.

"Brother, we keep running into these same two young ladies, what's up ladies," they all laughed.

"Same here."

"We are on our way to one of our barns to check on the tobacco."

"Boone, you all live in this area?" Kyra asked.

"Yes about five miles down the road."

Miles said, "That is why you need to know your neighborhood brother. You never know what may happen when you connect."

"What are you talking about?" asked Boone.

"Lizzie, I know your story, but I can change your story to our story." replied Miles.

Boone smiled at Kyra, "Okay ladies we have to get back on the road to work."

Miles said, "Wait Lizzie, can you and Kyra meet us at Wall Street, Friday night? I do not want to get you in trouble with your friend, so I will not ask to pick you up."

Boone said to Kyra, "I would love to meet with you also."

"See you all Friday night."

*****

The next morning, Philantha and Kyra are talking after breakfast. "Kyra, the bride and groom had their first born son. Cousin Bee was with the midwife to assist her, the baby was a healthy nine-pound boy. Cousin Bee said the quilt was so beautiful on their bed," said Philantha.

"Boone told me that he was a first time uncle when we were on the hayride. Mom, I like spending time with Boone," Kyra said.

"I can see the glow in your eyes when you say his name Kyra."

"Kyra, come help me with the clothes, they are clean and need to be transferred into the pot of rinse water. Wring them out, then pin them on the line," said Philantha. Kyra used the stick to pick the clothes out of one pot to the next pot because the water was still too hot to touch with her hands.

"Hello Kyra!" Rider said as he approached.

"Hello Rider, you need some help?" Kyra asked.

"I can always use help," Rider said as he went to touch the clothes Kyra set aside.

"Ouch! They are still hot!"

"Yes, allowing them to cool in the rinse water, then you can help pass me the clothes pins with some of the small pieces. Stay on that side of the rinse pot because the water is still very hot," Kyra explained.

"I can tell because you are sweating Kyra."

"Yes, I am Rider, so glad I have my hair in finger waves and wearing this scarf. Rider you are growing up so fast."

Rider replied, "I am ready to start school so I can ride the bus with Boe."

"When I started school, we had to walk to school every day in the rain"

"Really Kyra?"

"Yes, and the snow."

"Today, we have to go help Cousin Bee and her family with their tobacco. Polly, get your blanket so you can sit with Ammy," said Philantha.

"Mom, I want to help, you allow Rider to help," said Polly.

"You are helping when you take care of your sister Polly. Boe will be coming to get us soon. Kyra, can you bring some of those sausage biscuits for the girls? They may need something before dinner, I have some in the picnic basket."

"I am ready Mom."

*****

They arrived at Cousin Bee's barn and began helping. Lizzie pulled Kyra aside to talk.

"Kyra, we broke up last night," said Lizzie.

"What happened?" Kyra asked.

"I think he is seeing someone else and is confused at who he wants at this time, so we agreed to take some time away from each other," explained Lizzie.

"Lizzie how do you feel?" Kyra asked.

"I am content, and I feel free. I am young and I do desire to marry one day, but I want to be happy with my husband, and I desire the same for him. I will not settle for what I do not want in life."

"Life has a lot more to offer than just marriage," said Kyra.

"So true, each one of us has a different calling on our lives," said Lizzie.

"Girl, we need to enjoy our youth as much as we can. We can really enjoy Boone and Miles Friday night now."

"I am a little too anxious," said Kyra.

Lizzie, "You will be fine, trust me."

Polly ran up to Kyra, "Auntie Kyra, may Ammy and I have a biscuit, I am hungry."

"Yes Polly, Get them from the picnic basket."

"Here Ammy!" Polly said as she handed Ammy a biscuit.

"Thanks Polly, look on your back Polly what is it?" Ammy asked.

"Auntie get it off, get it off," screamed Polly.

"Stand still Polly", said Kyra. Rider pulled it off of Polly's top and she fell to the ground crying.

Rider was laughing out loud and said, "It is just a green tobacco worm that will not bite. Girls do not like any kind of bugs on or around them."

"I like bugs," said Ammy.

Polly said, "You are too young to know that bugs can and will bite."

Kyra was not about to touch the worm, so she said, "Thanks, Rider, for taking care of Polly."

"Polly is my twin for life. I will always be there for her, as well as little Ammy."

"Let's go, we are finished for today," said Boe,

"But we have to come back tomorrow to finish. The barns are full for today. The men have to take the cured tobacco out of one of the barns for tomorrow's harvest."

"Thanks family," said Cousin Bee.

"You are so welcome," said Philantha and Tilton as they all climbed on the wagon on the back of the tractor. Tilton rode on one of the big tires inside the wagon, beside Boe and Rider.

Boe said, "Papa I am glad we did not have another barn for today, this has been a long hard week."

"Yes, it has been Boe. Tomorrow will be a short day also," Papa said.

"Great! and it is Friday."

"Stop at the mailbox Boe, before you turn in the path," mom said.

"Okay, Mom." Rider jumped off of the tractor and pulled out the mail from the box.

"There was a package along with the mail," Rider told Philantha as he walked back.

Mom, "Who is the package from?"

"It is from Lang."

"Open it Grandmom, Mom said she would send Ammy and I a new tea set, maybe that is what's in the package." Philantha pulled the brown paper from the package and open the box. There were hair bows, headbands, bandana hankies, and scarves of different colors with two little doll babies wrapped separate. Gifts for everybody was written on the note. Polly and Ammy were jumping up and down with joy. Kyra gave the box to her mom so she could read the letter. Lang wrote:

Hey Kyra, I am living with one of the waitresses from my job. We have an efficiency apartment that we rent together. The rent is cheap, it works out good for us both. We spend most of our time at work, or out on the town. We found this club that is small, most of the people have gotten to know us. We go there at least twice during the week for happy hour, and then on the weekends. I think of you every time the music starts. I tell my friend that my sister would love this place, because of the music and the handsome men. Next week this jazz singer, named Billy Holiday, who is very popular at this club, will be performing, I am so excited Kyra. I've had the chance to see lots of famous singers and actors living in the city. I miss you so much I would love for you to visit. I cry myself to sleep at night thinking of Polly and Ammy. Time to turn the lights off, I have to work a double shift tomorrow. Kiss the girls and give everybody my love. See you soon, love Lang.

"Kyra, help me warm the dinner I only have to cook some corn bread."

"Mom, I am so happy for Lang. She said she moved in with a coworker and likes her new place. She misses everybody, and sends her love. Lang needs to come see the girls now it has been six months now," said Kyra.

"I heard Polly crying a few nights straight and when I went in, she told me that she misses her mom so much. Her crying woke Ammy, and then all three of us started crying," said Philantha.

Kyra asked, "Where was I Mom?"

"You had gone out with Lizzie. They both love to sleep with me, and I allow them to talk about what they love to do together. They fall asleep when I start talking about what I like," replied Philantha.

"I will write Lang tomorrow and tell her about how she really should come home soon."

# Chapter 13

# Bubba Visits Kyra

Late in the afternoon an unknown car was approached the house. Kyra and the girls were under the umbrella tree lying on a blanket, she was reading a book, while Rider was explaining to the girls the difference between each one of his soldiers.

Ammy said, "I want to be the Navy soldier, so I can ride in the boat." Kyra was so deep in her book she did not hear the car.

Rider had to shake her arm and ask, "Do you know who that is in that car?" The car stopped and Bubba stepped out of the car.

"Yes I know him Rider," said Kyra.

"Hello Kyra, I was in your neighborhood, so I just wanted to stop and speak with you."

"That's okay Bubba this is my brother Rider and my two nieces, Polly and Ammy."

Rider said, "Hello, did you know my birthday is the same day as Kyra's?"

"Wow no I did not, she never told me," Bubba replied.

"Oh, I told her friend Boone who I like a lot," said Rider.

"Great," Bubba said. "Let's go for a walk down the road."

Kyra replied, "Sounds good, I would love too. Girls, go in the house and tell Mom I am going for a walk and will be back soon."

"Can we go with you?" Ammy asked.

"Not this time girls," Kyra said as she and Bubba went for their walk. Rider was already in the house telling Boe about this young man.

"His name is not Boone," said Boe.

"Are you sure?" asked Rider.

Boe replied, "I know Boone when I see him, maybe it is just a close friend because I know she really does care for Boone."

Rider replied, "Okay."

After their walk Bubba said, "Kyra, I'll see you soon," as he walked to his car down the road. "Bye everyone."

"Bye," said Kyra.

Polly looked back at Kyra and said, "You have two boyfriends Auntie?"

"I have lots of friends Polly, but I do not call Bubba my boyfriend," Kyra said.

Rider said, "Polly that is because Boone is her boyfriend right Kyra?" Kyra smiled and took a deep breath and on the inside of that smile her heart was racing when Rider said Boone's name.

"I love you Rider, not sure about calling anyone my boyfriend."

"But Kyra, I can help you decide which one I like best."

"How can you do that?" she asked.

Rider replied, "I would pick the one that brings me a toy. Then I could be his friend and he could be your boyfriend."

Philantha walked outside, "Kyra the young man left?"

"Oh yes, Mom he just stopped to say hello. I did not want to disturb you."

"Have I met him?"

"Yes, Mom I introduced him to you and Papa when we were in town, his name is Bubba."

"Oh, I remember, nice young man."

"Not as nice as Boone," said Rider.

Kyra explained, "Mom, Rider has this thing for Boone."

"Okay Kyra, just like you right?" They laughed.

"Bubba will be leaving for the Navy in a few weeks, I am happy for him. He will be a great husband and father for a special young lady one day, but I just do not have the love for him that he deserves. I will always be a friend to him," said Kyra.

"Kyra, I am proud of the lady you are becoming, knowing what you want for yourself is very important, this is your life. Think it over good, he seems to be a smart one," said Philantha.

"Mom, my heart has been filled, and there is no more room for another young man at this time in my life. I really think I can live a lifetime and my heart will never be empty of this love I have for Boone," said Kyra.

"Those are some strong words lady."

"Kyra, today I have to go to Cousin Bee's house, I will be helping her with canning some fruit and she will come help me next week."

"Sounds like fun, you always seem to enjoy being with your cousin Bee," said Kyra.

"Yes, just like you when you are with Lizzie right?" Philantha asked.

"Yes, I love girl talk, we laugh so hard it hurts, and Cousin Bee has so much insight to offer about being a wife. I think I will take Polly and Ammy, early in the morning to the hen house to collect the eggs and then watch Papa cut up the hog. He will be making barbecue for the freezer."

"Okay, just make sure you keep them out of his way," said Philantha.

*****

They arrived at Cousin Bee's house and began canning fruits.

"Philantha, I have another young lady that I want us to bless with a quilt so we need to start getting the fabrics together, my desire for this one is to have the brightest colors as possible," said Cousin Bee.

"Bee, I have a lot of scraps from some fabric that I made dresses from the last two years for Polly and Ammy. I pray, I will not need any more baby clothes any time soon," said Philantha.

"You may have to save some for me," replied Bee.

"Who?" asked Philantha.

"Lizzie, I believe she is sexually active," Bee said.

"She told you?" Philantha replied.

"No but I can tell with her actions, she gives so much more attention to her looks," replied Bee.

Philantha said, "That is probably because she is close to Kyra and you know Kyra has always been mindful of her appearance as a little girl, since around three years old. She would say, Mom, I like those pretty colors and she loved to watch me comb and brush my hair."

"Okay if you say so, I pray that Lizzie waits to have children until she is married. Who is the quilt for we will be sewing?" Bee asked.

"It is a friend of the newlywed couple, she said her friend loved the one we made very much, so she asked me to see if the ladies would make one for her, and she would pay us. Her mom or grandmother never quilted. She was born and raised in the city and moved here with her husband. He is in the Navy and they are stationed here for a few years," replied Philantha.

"We love quilting so much, how can we charge?"

"Since her desire is bright colors, tell her to give you the money for the fabric and we will bless her and her husband with the quilt, because of their service to our country," replied Philantha.

"Maybe she can meet you the next time you go to town and pick out the colors of fabric that she desires."

"Sounds great."

# Chapter 14

# Kyra's Love Triangle

Papa and Boe, were cutting the hog in small pieces and adding the barbecue sauce that Philantha had made with vinegar, peppers and sugar.

"Papa can I taste that hog too?"

"Taste good Auntie Kyra?"

"Yes, Polly, give Ammy some too. Kyra can you bring me the freezer bags from that large box on the table? Then start packing the meat in each bag with Rider while Boe and I finish seasoning the other half of the hog."

"Yes Sir."

"Rider, come clean your hands in the wash pan with me, and here is a large spoon that you can use to pick up the meat."

"Kyra, this hog is so good. I need some bread."

"Rider you are eating more than you are packing."

"I will not need dinner."

"If Papa catches you eating, you will not get supper today or tomorrow.

Rider laughed and said, "You're right."

Lizzie walked in the kitchen, "Hello Cousin Philantha."

"Hello Lizzie. You came to help?"

Lizzie replied, "Yes, I have been in the pack house getting more jars for you all to use."

"Clean them for me Lizzie, and then you can help finish peeling the peaches, and the pears are cooking."

"Yes, Mom it smells good in here."

"Kyra and I are going out tonight, we are meeting two brothers at Wall Street," said Lizzie.

Philantha asked, "Why are you meeting them, and why are they not driving you all as their date?"

Lizzie explained, "Well at the time, I had a boyfriend when I was asked out, but as of last week I am a single and open to date others."

"Sounds as if you may have been single when he asked you, or you would not have agreed on a date."

"Cousin Philantha, we had not been getting along for months. My feeling had changed toward him after I met this young man. I was just talking with him and nothing else, he makes me feel like a lady. Kyra helped me understand what I wanted and needed in a boyfriend. I will not settle for disrespect and control from anyone," said Lizzie.

"I am so proud of how Kyra will not settle for anything in so many areas of her life. She can be stubborn at times, but she will not compromise her beliefs."

"Kyra, we will have some of the barbecue with supper tonight, just warm a bowl full. I have some leftover rabbit to warm, that will be our meat," said Philantha.

"Mom I like cornbread with my barbecue. Can you cook some? I am cutting white potatoes to boil with the cabbage," said Kyra. Polly and Ammy walked in the kitchen.

"Hello girls." They were covered in dirt, "What happen to you two?" asked Philantha.

"We were swinging in the tire on the tree and we fell a few times in the dirt. It was so much fun we could not stop."

Philantha said, "But you know better Polly, than to get you and your sister's hair dirty."

"Sorry Grandmom," said Polly.

"Take the plaits out of Ammy's hair and then yours. You cannot sleep in the bed with all those grits of dirt in your hair."

"Mom, I am glad it is Friday because I was going to clean their hair tomorrow anyway."

"Well, I am going to get as much of the grits out as possible. Then I will tie a scarf on their hair until you can give them a bath from head to toe tomorrow; that is too much hair for me tonight."

"Yes, because I am going out tonight with Lizzie, we are meeting our dates at the club."

"Yes, she told me already."

Papa walked in the kitchen and said, "Whose dirt balls are these little girls?"

Ammy said, "Papa's dirt balls."

Everybody laughed and Polly said, "I am Aunt Kyra's dirt ball."

"Get out of the kitchen, dirt balls," replied Tilton.

"Come on Ammy, let me take your plaits out, and mine before dinner. Then we will clean our face and hands," said Kyra.

Philantha said, "Do not forget to dust the dirt off your clothes."

*****

Lizzie and Kyra drove up in the parking lot, and Boone and Miles were sitting in their car waiting to walk the ladies in the club. As they walked in the club the band was playing, but Bubba was not on stage. The leader of the band stood up after the band stopped playing and asked for everyone's attention. Bubba walked from the back of the club.

"I would like us all to thank Bubba for his contribution to our band and this club. He is beginning a new journey in his life as an enlisted sailor in the Navy, and service member for our country. Bubba would you like to say anything to the people?"

"I have fully enjoyed my journey as a member of this band as a young man. Wall Street has allowed me to connect with some great people and I would like to thank you all for your friendship. I especially want to thank Kyra, a young lady that I adore and respect greatly and would love to continue our friendship in the future. Kyra please come to the front."

Kyra looked at Boone, and Boone looked puzzled. Kyra stood up and walked to the stage. Lizzie dropped her head and Boone walked out of the club. Afterwards, Kyra met Lizzie at the car.

"What would you have done if that had been you Lizzie?" asked Kyra.

"I would have asked Boone if he was okay with me going to the stage. Instead, you just walked off without a word. You were on a date Kyra. When Miles walked me to the car, he told me that Boone was embarrassed, and felt like you were not open with your feelings about Bubba.

"I told him you did not feel the same way for Bubba as he did for you. But he will not say anything to Boone because that is your relationship." Miles walked out with Boone to make sure he was okay, but Boone would not come back in the club."

Kyra said, "Lizzie, I feel like the love scents in my heart are draining to my stomach and causing it to ache because of the pain I feel. I disappointed the very one that I love."

"Kyra, so you said it?"

"Yes, I know. I love Boone."

Weeks had passed since Kyra's date with Boone. Bubba had left for training and no word from Boone.

## Chapter 15

## Lang Comes Home to Visit

"Kyra!! That same car that Lang left in with brother is coming up the path." Polly ran out of the house, followed by Ammy.

Boe said, "Mom Lang is here; tell Papa." Lang could hardly wait for the car to stop. Polly and Ammy jumped in her arms and everyone was crying and laughing at the same time.

"Wow I have only been gone for six months and you two are all legs."

"Mom, I love your dress you look so pretty," said Ammy. Polly said nothing, she just held on to Lang's hand.

"Hello Mom, hello Papa."

They all smiled and said, "It is good to see you Lang." They were not huggers, but Kyra hugged Lang tight.

"I missed you so much more than you will ever know." Rider had so many questions for Lang. Boe smiled and told jokes and had everybody laughing.

"Mom, how long will you be home?"

"Ammy, I plan to stay for three days," replied Lang.

"Great, we have a lot to talk about." Then Ammy turned to Philantha, "Grandmom, let me bring the clothes off the line and help Polly dry the dishes, and then I can talk with Mom," said Ammy.

"Polly why are you so quiet?" asked Lang.

"I cannot believe you came back," replied Polly.

"I am sorry it has been such a long time," Lang said as she hugged Polly. "I really did not want to ride the bus, so I waited until brother had a few days off from his job." Lang turned to Kyra, "When the girls go to sleep, we will talk Kyra."

"I understand Lang, they need this time with you."

"Girls, let's go help Mom and Kyra with supper."

"Okay I love to cook," said Polly.

"You can cook?" asked Lang.

"Yes, I stir the soup in the big bowl, but I still cannot clean the bowl, because grand mom does not want me to drop her favorite bowl, so she always cleans the bowl. Ammy loves to lick the bowl after Grandmom and I mix the cake batter."

"Mom, I like to listen to Rider tell me about some of the stories Boe, read to him. I am not a cook. I will clean up before I cook."

"You girls are growing up so fast. Rider and I will start school soon, Ammy is still too little."

"Ammy, you do not have long before you will start school. Until then you can help Grandmom keep the house clean."

"Yes Mom, I will."

Philantha called out, "Supper is ready."

"Ammy, go tell Papa he can come eat."

"Okay Grandmom, I know I will have to wake him up, because he says he is looking at the TV, but he is always nodding."

"Yes, your Papa will nod if he gets quiet and still."

"Papa! Papa! Come eat."

"Okay Ammy." Lang shared her time away with the family and they all listened.

"Mom, I will help you and Kyra clean the kitchen, how are you?" asked Lang.

"Busy all the time. The girls are a lot. Kyra helps me so much with them I could not keep up without her. Remember Rider and Polly are the same age and then Ammy is younger. Children are different from when you and Kyra were young, but you need to thank your sister for raising your girls with me, because she will stay home if I am not feeling well and keep the girls when she would much rather go to her favorite place," replied Philantha.

"Speaking of favorite place, tomorrow is Friday," said Kyra.

"That is why I came on a Thursday Kyra."

"I do not know why but, she has missed a few weeks from going anywhere. Maybe she will talk to you Lang."

"Okay Mom, I will ask her." Kyra looked away and changed the subject.

"Lang, Cousin Lizzie and I have grown close since you left, but she could never take your place. I am so glad I have her to talk with, and she has learned to dance, and she loves Wall Street club. Aunt Bee never would allow her to go to clubs until she started spending time with me. Lizzie never desired to dance. Lizzie and I were in a dance contest, and you know we were the favorite pick. The judges allowed the club goers to choose the winner based on the loudest clap or noise."

"Kyra, I am glad you are enjoying life with Lizzie. Tell me more about your relationship with Boone." Kyra turned her back to Lang.

"Kyra are you crying?" She took Lang's hand.

"Can we go for a walk please?" Kyra told the story to Lang about the last time she saw Boone at the club and how Bubba should have had more respect for Boone in front of all the people that she knows and love.

"Kyra, Bubba loves you, so he was expressing his heart and he did not care who knew."

"Lizzie told me, I should have said more to Boone myself. Pondering over that night in my mind, I should have asked Boone, if he was okay with me going to the stage. Bubba was just thanking his friends and wanted to give a special thanks to me. I cannot imagine how Boone felt in front of all those people, he was so hurt and confused about our relationship and his brother Miles said he felt like I had been lying to him. I never once told Boone about Bubba's feelings for me, because I was afraid Boone would not desire a relationship with me. Lang, I have not seen or spoken with Boone since that night and it hurts so much. Love can be a hurting emotion, a painful experience, overwhelming feeling of disconnect. Lang how would you approach Boone? Lizzie offered to drive me to Boone's house."

"Kyra, you have to allow Boone to come to you, if that is what he wants. Put some time on it, the pain is a part of the time, okay."

"Lang, I miss our times together especially when I am crying myself to sleep."

"Kyra, I have had a few heartbreaks myself, but you will heal. I pray you and Boone can come together and talk about your feelings for each other and not allow this one bad experience to destroy the closeness you two have had for over a year."

# Chapter 16

# Boone Joins the Navy

"Lizzie will be here soon Lang," said Kyra.

"I finally got Polly and Ammy to sleep, they would not stop talking. I have a gift for you, Kyra. I brought you this blue dress, I hope you like the high collar and ruffles." Lang looked at the ruffles on the collar and the buttons on the sleeves and handed it to Kyra.

"Wow Lang, I love it, I am changing into this beautiful dress, so I can model for you. It is just my length; you know your sister's taste in clothes very well. I have short navy blue boot shoes that will go good with this length. Lang what are you wearing?" asked Kyra.

Lang pulls a white dress from her suitcase. "Look at this white dress, the dress has red ruffles on the bottom and there are zippers on the sleeves that I adore."

"I have never seen zippers on the sleeve of a dress," said Kyra.

"Kyra the fashions are so different in the city than here in the sticks. The ruffles will match my red lips, girl."

"Lang you know Mom can make any of these dresses, just get her the right fabrics and a pattern, and it is done."

"So now we can dress to impress, we will get all the attention on Wall Street," they both laughed and finished applying the red lipstick. They got dressed and waited for Lizzie.

"Ladies you both look lovely. Kyra where did you get that beautiful dress?" asked Philantha.

"This is a city dress Mom!" said Kyra as she showed off her dress.

"Yes, it is Kyra, and you, Lang look like a city girl in that pretty white dress," said Philantha.

"Thanks Mom. Did you like your gifts?"

"Yes! Lang, I did not think you would remember my shoe size. The shoes fit perfect and I love my patent leather pocketbook. The soft pink, blue, and cream satin fabrics are beautiful," replied Philantha.

"What will you make from that fabric Mom?"

"I was thinking of purchasing a different blouse pattern, more of a fancy type for you Kyra, but I will make me an under garment for myself, because I like the smooth feel of the fabric on my skin."

"Can you make me a slip also Mom?"

"Yes Kyra."

"Mom, I am glad you like your fabric as a gift, it is hard to purchase outfits for you because you love to sew."

"Lang, I did not think Mom will like the city dresses," said Kyra. They laughed out loud and enjoyed their conversation until they heard a car horn. Lizzie picked up Lang and Kyra then they all went to Wall Street.

"Ladies you two look like movie stars tonight. You remember Elizabeth Taylor in the movie *Little Women* with June Allyson, you two are dressed for success. Your outfits, hair, and the makeup are beautiful, just like the ladies in the movie," said Lizzie.

"Thank you, Lizzie, you look wonderful yourself," replied Lang.

"Lang, Kyra has helped me so much with my mindset and my outlook on life and you know my choice of clothes and my hair," said Lizzie.

"I hardly knew you when you approached me, you have always been a beautiful young lady. I think Kyra just helped bring out of you what was dormant on the inside of you Lizzie, and now it shows in more than one way," said Lang.

"Thanks Lang how are you?" said Lizzie.

"I am good, glad to be home with Kyra," replied Lang. When the ladies walked in the club all eyes turned on them. The club was long in length with only six tables that seats six people. If you got there late, you had to stand against the wall. When you walked in the club, the band was right next to the front door entrance, and everyone had to pass the band to get to their seats. The dance floor was tight, with little room for everyone to dance at the same time. This made it more fun to take a break from dancing, and stand back to watch others on the floor. Lang, Kyra, and Lizzie caught the eye of everyone in the club that night with their astounding beauty.

"Kyra, look at how everyone is smiling at us," replied Lang as they approached the table to the right of the band. Lang was speaking to the people at the next table as they took their seats.

"Lang it is because of you, that they are speaking, well it sure feels good," said Kyra. Miles approached the lady's table.

"Hello Ladies, hello Lizzie. May I join you?"

"Yes Miles."

"Lang, come dance with me." Kyra took Lang's hand and said, "I think Lizzie likes Miles, so I wanted them to be alone for a few moments."

As they danced Lang said, "I thought you would be more anxious of why Boone was not with him."

"I know Lizzie will ask him, so I did not want to be the one to ask about Boone. When I say his name, I can feel the tears forming in my mind." They danced and then went back to sit down.

Miles looked at Kyra and said, "I guess you would not know but Boone joined the Navy and was shipped out now two weeks." Lang squeezed Kyra hand under the table. "The last time you all were together he planned to tell you Kyra and more, but in all the confusion he chose not to tell you." Kyra's heart ached as she looked into Miles eyes.

"Can you please give me Boone's address?" asked Kyra.

"He would love to hear from you, I know he misses you Kyra. Before I leave tonight, I will get the address from my car."

"Thanks Miles."

"Lizzie may I have this dance?" asked Miles as he took Lizzie's hand and went to the dance floor.

"Lang why did he have the address in his car?" asked Kyra.

"Miles knew he would see you tonight," replied Lang.

"Lang, is that your baby's dad right beside us at 3:00?"

"Oh my God! Yes, and that is the young lady he married with him."

"Will you speak with him?" asked Kyra.

"No Kyra, when he denied Polly, I just said cut it. Polly, has Papa now and one day if she asks me, I will tell her the story of how she was conceived."

Lizzie walked with Miles to his car. "Lizzie you look so lovely tonight."

"Thanks Miles."

"Since Boone left home, I have to make some different moves myself. I plan to move to another state soon." Miles pulled her to him and gave her a passionate kiss.

"Come lay with me Lizzie because I may never see you again."

"Miles, I care a lot for you, and I've had great times with you, but we are not in love with each other," said Lizzie."

"I respect you Lizzie. Are you sure?"

"Yes, I am Miles." Kyra walked to Miles car to get Boone's address.

"Thanks, Miles, for the address,"

"You're welcome Kyra, take care ladies, goodnight." Lang and Kyra were talking on their way home and Lizzie was very quiet.

"Lizzie did you not enjoy your night with Miles?"

"Miles asked me to lie with him tonight, but I turned him down. My body aches still now for him, I told him we were not in love with each other.

I wanted him to say I love you Lizzie, or I do care for you a lot. He just said he has plans to move to another state soon and may never see me again.
That was not enough for me, I knew I would just miss him more, so I turned him down. Miles awakens my love scents every time we meet. I will miss him."

"Lizzie, life is so full of change, be encouraged, we have to take it one day at a time."

"Yes, we will always remember this, no matter what or where we are in life."

"Thanks Lang, I am so glad you are my sister."

"Yes, thanks cousin. Tonight was very interesting with all three of us, replied Lizzie.

The next day, Lang is prepared to return to the city. Brother's car is packed and Lang said her goodbyes to Kyra, Ammy and Polly.

"Write us tomorrow okay, we love you so much," said Ammy. The girls were holding both her hands. Lang kissed them both and turned and walked to the car with tears in her eyes. The girls were still waving as the car went out of there sight.

Polly took Ammy by the hand and said, "Sister, I love you, and when we grow up, we will always stay together."

Kyra said, "Girls come show me your paper dolls and we can dress them in a new outfit."

# Chapter 17

# Family Time at the Fair

The next few weeks everybody was busy preparing the kids for school again, and harvesting of the crops. Boe was excited about going back to school. Rider and Polly walked with Boe to the bus stop as long as the weather was warm. Later in the year, they waited for him on the porch.

"Lizzie is out front Auntie Kyra."

"Hello, I stopped to ask you if you would like to go to the fair."

"I was going with Papa to take the girls, but I prefer an adult day out at the fair. So, Rider and Boe can help him, and Mom is going so they will be just fine without me."

"Mom, I will be going with Lizzie to the fair, maybe we will see each other there."

"Kyra go and enjoy yourself with your friends."

This young man almost stepped on Lizzie foot and said, "Hello." She looked up and there was her ex-boyfriend.

"Lizzie! Hello, can I speak with you alone?"

"Kyra excuse me for a moment."

"I will wait here on this bench for you." Kyra walked away and headed to a different spot at the fair. As she walked she spotted Miles.

"Miles! Good to see you."

"Hi Kyra, how are you?"

"I am well."

"You here alone?"

"No, Lizzie is with me."

"Lizzie, yea, where is she?"

"She'll be back soon."

There was a young lady with Miles. "This is my friend."

"Nice to meet you," said Miles' friend,

Miles asked, "Kyra have you heard from Boone yet?"

"No," Kyra replied with sadness in her heart.

"You know he told me you wrote him. Tell Lizzie I said hello." Miles walked away, and Lizzie still was not back. Kyra waited and waited. So, Kyra decided to play a game and get her a hotdog, then went back to the bench and wait for Lizzie. Philantha, saw Kyra seated and went over to her.

"Kyra why are you alone?"

"I'm waiting for Lizzie, but I think I will find some friends and ride until she decides to come back."

"Papa and I are leaving the park, see you when you get home," said Philantha before leaving. Kyra enjoyed the fair with friends, but she was concerned about Lizzie being gone for so long. It was getting dark; Kyra and a few friends walked to the outside bathroom. She passed this car and there was Lizzie with her ex-boyfriend hugging and kissing. Kyra walked away and waited until they were done until finding Lizzie again.

"Lizzie, I saw you in the car and why was he all over you? I thought..."

Lizzie interuppted saying, "Kyra I am okay, and I did not mean to be gone so long. Are you ready to leave?"

Weeks passed and Lizzie did not stop by Kyra's house, and that was not the norm. One day, Kyra decided she was going to check on Lizzie.

"Mom I am going to walk to see Lizzie. Can the girls walk with me?" asked Kyra. Kyra and the girls arrived at Lizzie's house.

"Girls play with Lizzie's sister while we talk okay." Kyra went inside to talk to Lizzie. "I miss you Lizzie. Are you okay?"

"Kyra I allowed my feelings to take over at the fair, and I had sex with him. I am so ashamed and disappointed in myself. I know he does not love me, but I love him."

"Remember we take it one day at a time," said Kyra.

"I love you so much Kyra."

"Cousin, you are my wingwoman, and I am yours." Kyra and the girls went home and Papa brought the mail from the mailbox.

"Kyra you have a letter. It looks as if the address was wrong because someone scratched it out and wrote the correct one. They must have known your name."

"Thanks Papa, is it from Lang?" Kyra took the letter and as she looked at the address and she knew it was from Boone.

# Chapter 18

# Kyra Recieves a Letter from Boone

Kyra ran outside to walk down the path as she opened the letter. Boone wrote:

> Kyra, I think of you day and night, I dream of you during the day and when I go to sleep at night. I received your letter and I feel the same way about you. I am sorry I did not tell you that I was leaving. I did not know how you felt about Bubba, and I did not want to know at that time. So please forgive me. I had planned that night to tell you I was leaving and to also ask you if you would be my girl and wait for me."

Kyra dropped the letter. Tears of joy were flooding Kyra's eyes and heart. Kyra continued to read the letter over and over again, that night she slept with the letter under her pillow. The next morning before she could eat, Kyra wrote Lang and told her of the wonderful news.

"Mom, Boone wrote me as you know, but I could not talk about it. I was so full that I was at lost for words. All I wanted to do was read his words and feel the love. Every word on the pages was flowing over and over in my heart, as if Boone was right beside me."

"Kyra I am so happy for you. What did he ask you that you need to tell me?" asked Philantha.

"Boone asked me to be his girl and if I would wait for him."

*****

Months passed and Kyra wrote to Boone every week. Boone could not write as often as Kyra because he was out to sea on the ship. He talked about how he was one of the cooks, and the large amount of food they had to cook every day. Kyra looked forward to Boone's letters as he would tell her of his adventures at sea. Lizzie was with child, 9 months any day now, and Kyra was her support.

"I am getting excited about our baby; I want a boy," said Kyra.

"Kyra, you are funny, you want my baby to be a boy. Mom said, she believes I am caring a boy. Kyra, I just think of my child not having a father in the home."

"Your child will be a great blessing for you, and your dad will be the child's dad for now."

Lizzie had a healthy baby boy that brought her much joy. She named him Hagan, meaning distinguished, pleasant to look upon, light of the morning after the rain.

"Thanks, Kyra for all your support to me and Hagan."

Kyra was reading a letter from Boone. He had been gone now two years, and he was telling her his time was almost up. He would be coming home in a few months. Lang was also in love, sharing her letters with Kyra. Both girls were in love and excited about their future.

# Chapter 19

# Kyra Becomes Boone's Wife

Polly and Rider were of age now to start school for the upcoming school year. Philantha was preparing for Thanksgiving. Tilton chose one of the turkeys to fatten up to be killed for Thanksgiving dinner.

"Papa, that is a large turkey. I like turkey meat with Grandmom's cornbread stuffing. Ammy and I will help you with the sweet potatoes from the barn."

"Okay, come with me," said Tilton.

"I will miss helping you on the farm everyday Papa, because you know I am a big girl now and I will be in school all day soon. Ammy will have to help you more, right Ammy?" She smiled and shook her head. Christmas was just a few weeks away. Kyra was helping with the hollies that Philantha hung on the doors in the house.

"There are two cars coming toward the house. One is Lang and brother, but I do not recognize the other vehicle," said Boe. Polly and Ammy were jumping up and down. Kyra and Philantha walked out on the porch. Papa was in the rocking chair, everybody was waiting, even Old Yeller, the dog. The first car parked, and Lang, with her friend stepped out. Then brother stepped out. The second car parked, and out stepped Miles and then Boone.

"Boone! What a surprise," said Kyra. They took each other by the hand.

"Yes, Kyra I wanted to be your Christmas surprise," said Boone.

"Well, I love my surprise," replied Kyra.

"Everybody, in the house, dinner will be served soon," said Philantha.

"Miles, I thought you moved to the city," said Kyra.

"I did but I am home for Christmas. My friend is at home with my Mom. I would not have missed this reunion for anything," said Miles.

"Yes, I would love for you to meet my family later today Kyra," said Boone.

"Okay, Boone. I would love to meet your family," said Kyra.

They talked and talked, and then Lang and her friend decided to take Boone home. They all met Boone's family and Boone's family met Kyra and Lang.

Boone's dad said, "I have known your mom and dad for years. I have seen you all with them in town and at church, nice meeting you both." Boone's Mom was a petite lady that spoke softly and smiled all the time.

Kyra said, "Boone, I know where you got your good looks from, your handsome father."

"Yes you know a good looking man when you see one." They both laughed.

Everyone talked for awhile and then Lang, her friend, Kyra, Boone and Miles decided to spend their first night together on Wall Street. They arrived and the club was packed with laughter and music.

The song, "The Man I Love" started playing, and Kyra looked at Boone, he took her by the hand, and they walked out on the dance floor together. Kyra melted in his arms.

Boone smiled at her and said, "Kyra, will you be my wife?"

Kyra looked at Boone and said, "Yes, I would love to be your wife."

*****

The wedding was a dream come true for Kyra and Boone. The sounds of laughter filled the cold air. Smiles were on all the guest faces. Kyra and Boone stood holding hands as the pastor spoke to each one of them. Kyra's mind went back in time when she told Lang about her desire to have a man with a slow hand as she squeezed Boone's hand. The dimples on Boone's face, were bigger than ever. The expression on both their faces showed how deep their love was for each other.

Kyra was dressed in a mid-length, light blue dress with a wide collar. The dress had ruffles around the bottom of the collar with white buttons down the front of the dress. The earrings matched the white buttons on the dress. Her white stockings and white low heel shoes brought out the beauty of the dress. Kyra's hair was combed to one side, pinned up with long black curls, which made her look like a princess being swept away by the love of her life. Boone wore a loose white shirt with a belt that he wore over the bottom of the shirt. It covered the top of his gray dress pants with a white watch on his arm and gray loafer shoes. Boone had a head of black curls himself. The entire wedding scenery looked as if a prince and princess were getting married.

The pastor said you may now kiss your bride; Kyra's love scents were flowing like waves as Boone kissed her lips. Everybody was happy for Kyra and Boone. Miles and Lang were so relieved with joy you would have thought they were the parents.

The guest were eating and the music was playing, Lang and Miles were telling stories of how Kyra and Boone met, and the good times they had together on Wall Street. Kyra and Boone sat quietly and laughed, listening to Lang and Miles, while holding hands.

During Kyra and Boone's first night together, they went to sleep holding each other and when they awoke Kyra was still in Boone's arms. Boone woke up.

"Kyra, I love you."

"I love you Boone, I cannot believe we are husband and wife; I am happy Boone to be your wife. I do not want to get out of bed right now because you and this quilt feels so good to me. Boone, it is just 5am, we do not have to get up now." They made love again and fell fast asleep.

"Kyra what time is it now?"

"Still early Boone." Kyra was watching Boone sleep, and their first day began with coffee and breakfast in bed.

"Let's open the other gifts Boone."

"Okay, sounds good." Philantha had quilted Kyra and Boone a quilt with the help of the ladies. Polly and Ammy promised not to tell Kyra and they kept their word.

Kyra and Boone's wedding was six months after he was honorably discharged from the Navy in July 27, 1946. Boone was in the navy two years, and his duty was a cook on the ship as he served our country. He served his time and then came home to marry his love, Kyra. It was on a Wednesday afternoon, January 15th, 1947 when their union began.

## Chapter 20

# Boone and Kyra's First Child

The wind was blowing hard and large snowflakes were falling from the sky. Kyra was cooking and Boone was outside splitting firewood to stack on the porch, because the snow was covering the wood in the yard, Boone did not want to have to dig the wood out of the snow.

"Boone! Boone!" The wind was so loud, he could hardly hear Kyra.

"Do you need help?"

"You can take some of the small pieces in the house and place them in the woodbox."

"Kyra, this is a snowstorm, the wind was blowing snow all over the porch, the swing was full of snow. I had to clean the porch before I could stack the wood, who knows how many inches will fall before it stops."

"Well, we will be warm and cozy for a week or two with all that wood you cut. I want you to be warm."

"Breakfast smells good, my favorite hog brains with eggs, fried apples, fatback meat and biscuits."

"Boone what are your plans today?"

"I will walk to Mom and Dads to see if Dad needs any help with wood or the animals. I will not move the truck in this snow."

"Okay, I will dress warm and walk with you, I am glad we live close."

"We live so close, I could see the smoke coming from their chimney when I was cutting the wood earlier," said Boone.

"The newlyweds are here, Boone's youngest brother called out to his dad."

"Hello, family, surprised to see you all so early."

"Yes, I wanted to see if you needed help with the animals or wood dad."

"Yes, can you move the block of salt for Betsy, closer to the shed? I have to feed the mules, and I have plenty of wood on the porch."

"How is married life son, it has been a month now?"

"Kyra and I are getting to know each other because I can be shy at times. Dad, I almost burned my butt bathing beside the heater trying to keep warm, because I did not want Kyra to see me naked. Kyra laughed and laughed, and then I laughed because it was not that serious."

"Son you will get over that shyness soon. Learn to listen to your wife. Do not tell her but, wives are right most of the time. Listening can lead to so much peace in the home. Women need to know that we are interested in what they are saying, even if you are not in agreement, listen son."

Months passed and the March winds were blowing. The rain was falling and the air was crisp.

"Kyra where are the seeds that your Papa gave us to plant?"

"Look on the shelf on the back porch, they are still in the bags."

"We will plant them in containers so the seeds can germinate. We'll keep them on the porch until it is time to plant them in the garden."

"Boone, I think I have a seed germinating, that you planted a few weeks ago."

"Kyra!! I love you; I love you."

"Boone we will have our first child, Spring is coming!"

*****

Kyra woke up with Lang on her mind. "Boone, I will write Lang today; I want her to be the first one that I tell of our good news."

"Why not write Miles and let him be the second person."

"Kyra, we will go see your mom and papa to tell them in person this weekend."

"Okay, so how will you keep that from your dad when you see him today?" asked Kyra.

"I am not sure how yet," replied Boone.

Kyra went to the store and ran into Lizzie and Hagan.

"Lizzie who is this big boy?" asked Kyra.

"Hello, Cousin Kyra." He gave her a big hug,

"Hagan, you have grown so much."

"Kyra, how is married life?"

"I am so happy with my husband, my heart scents flow all day long with him."

"Girl, that must be a wonderful feeling, I am so happy for you and Boone." Boone came out of the shoe repair store.

"Hello, Lizzie good to see you and Hagan."

"Did you tell Lizzie?" asked Boone.

"Not yet, we just approached each other as you walked out of the store. Boone, I have to get some fabric for Mom, and then I will be ready."

"Tell me what?"

"Kyra is with child; my Kyra will be a mother soon." Lizzie hugged Kyra and they both cried and laughed.

"Our children can grow up together, and Hagan will be the protector as the oldest, you know his name means strong defense and Immovable."

Philantha and Tilton were sitting outside under the umbrella tree, the boys were playing catch, and Polly and Ammy were playing with their paper dolls on a blanket.

Rider said, "Look, it's Kyra and Boone."

"Hello family, looks like you all are having a quiet afternoon."

The girls ran to give Kyra a hug and Rider said, "Hello Kyra and Boone, can you play catch with Boe and me?"

"Just a second Rider, we have some good news. Kyra, and I will have an addition to our family soon, around Christmas time."

Everybody smiled and Papa said, "That was fast."

"Auntie Kyra we will have a cousin to play with, I want a girl to play with."

Polly said, "Me too Ammy."

Philantha said, "Great, I see the quilt is working for you and Boone too."

"Yes"

"Mrs. Philantha, you know my sister that you ladies made the quilt for? She has three children already. It will not surprise me if she is not with child on this very day. She just pushes them out and tells everybody once they are born," said Boone.

"Mom, I purchased some fabric and brought it today with me so you could make me a few dresses and tops when you have some free time."

"Now is a good time before spring comes, which is seed time and a busy time of the year for farmers."

"Thanks Mom, I am so excited about my first child, and a little scared."

"You will be just fine, you already have plenty of practice with your nieces," said Philantha.

"Yes, have you heard from Lang? I should get a letter this week. Polly and Rider will be attending school in August and I need her to buy Polly's coat, boots, and shoes. I need to tell her now so she can save money for those items. I purchased different colors of fabric to make Polly's dresses, skirts, and tops. Polly is so excited about starting school and Rider just wants to ride the bus with Boe.

# Chapter 21

# Birthday and Christmas Celebration

Boone and Kyra's garden produced plenty of vegetables last summer to pack, freeze, and can for the winter months ahead.

"Boone, can you help pick some more apples before they rot? I want them to freeze some, and I want to get some so Mom and I can preserve them. Rider loves Apple preserve, so I have to have plenty when he comes to stay."

"Kyra get some rest."

"I feel good Boone, thanks, I will rest after dinner."

"I will get Rider and Polly to help me with the apple picking tomorrow since they are out of school for the summer."

"Kyra, you finally gained some weight now, I can tell you are with child."

"I feel fat Mom."

"You will never be fat girl. You only have a couple months."

"Lang, thanks for the gown and the beautiful housecoat," said Kyra.

"You need it Kyra, you are moving really slowly since my last visit, not long before you deliver," said Lang.

"Polly, look at Riders new fire truck he got for Christmas." Ammy was hugging her new stuffed teddy bear; everybody was talking and having fun around the Christmas tree.

"Can we sing Happy Birthday to Mom while I am here since it is only a few days away?"

"Kyra are you feeling okay?" asked Boone's mom.

"Mom, Kyra did not sleep well last night. She turned and twisted in bed all night," said Boone.

"Since it is late afternoon, why don't you stay for the night, I can keep an eye on her, the baby could come any day now."

"Thanks Mom, because I will not know what to do alone with Kyra." Boone went home to get some items of clothing that Kyra requested, and some PJ's for himself.

Kyra went into labor later that night, and gave birth to a baby girl.

"Spring is here, she is a bundle of joy. Rider and I share the same birthday. Spring and my Mom also share the same birthday," said Kyra.

"That is amazing."

"Boone, I thank your mom for helping and teaching me how to take care of Spring the first month of her life, and all the good meals we shared together being in your parent's home."

"Boone are you happy? I knew you talked about having a son."

"Kyra, I am thankful for a healthy precious little girl. She just came first; we will have boys and girls."

"Yes, I pray that we will too Boone."

*****

Months passed and Spring is almost one year old. Kyra and Boone take Spring to visit Philantha. Polly and Ammy were excited to play with Spring.

"Polly and Ammy would love it if you came everyday Kyra," said Philanta.

"Auntie Kyra, Spring laughs when we play patty cake," said Polly.

"Polly, she loves attention all the time, I think her dad has spoiled her and everybody else."

"Time for a nap girls. Yes Ammy, she can lay on the blanket with you and Polly." After spending the day together with her family, Boone picked up Kyra and Spring. Snow was falling as they rode home.

It was Spring's first birthday, the fireplace was cracking and the music was playing. Spring was full of laughter around the house.

"Spring's birthday is just a few days before yours, Boone. I cooked your favorite meal, and we can sing Happy Birthday to you and Spring after we eat. Last year, Spring was your birthday gift. I cannot wait, open your gift now."

"You bought me a harmonica? Thanks, Kyra, for your love and my gifts."

Spring fell asleep and Kyra and Boone enjoyed the night together talking about how they met. From the beginning of their friendship, they both had strong feelings that they could not be explained.

"Boone, I love you but you do not talk about your feelings."

"Kyra, yes you are more open with your feelings than I am, but always remember I love myself some Kyra." Boone held her tight as they passionately made love.

"Good morning, I plan to go visit my sister today. Last week she asked me to purchase a toy that Spring had the last time we were there, this is her fourth child. I am an uncle, so I want to spend more time with her children and also Spring can play with her cousins," said Boone.

"Wow, I think we may need to stop sleeping under our quilt Boone, your sister has had a child every year since she was married. It is the quilt, the ladies prayed that they would have a quiver full, and that prayer is manifesting every year," said Kyra.

"I wonder what words were spoken with the one they gave to us, Kyra."

"Boone, I want a small quiver."

"Are you and Spring, coming with me?"

"What about the snow?" asked Kyra.

"There is no more than two inches on the ground. We will be just fine in the truck," said Boone.

"Then we can go straight to Mom's house for Sunday dinner."

"Thanks, Mom, for dinner. I went to see my youngest niece today."

"Great."

"Your sister brought her to see me last week. She is a few weeks older than Spring right?"

"Yes, about eight weeks."

"Spring enjoys playing with her cousin."

"My family is growing fast; I have five grands Boone."

"Kyra and I will make that number as high as we can Mom," replied Boone.

"Boone you are just talking, Kyra is not ready for another child."

"We will try for our boy very soon." Kyra was listening and just smiled as she spoke to her inner self, he really wants a boy and I love Boone so much, I want to carry his son if that will bring him joy.

"Kyra will that bring you joy?"

"Sure Mom."

"Boone you ready to leave, can we check on my Mom and Papa, I have a new belt I brought for Rider that he needs for school." As Rider looked from the window, he could hear the truck coming up the path to the house.

"Hey everyone." Rider took Spring from Boone's arms and started tickling her so that she would laugh.

"Kyra, is the snow melting on the highway?" asked Papa.

"Yes dad, we had no problems driving today at all." Philantha was in the kitchen preparing supper. "Mom, you need help?" asked Kyra.

"Yes, I miss you helping me so much, but I am happy you have your own family."

"What is that noise?"

"Sounds like Polly and Ammy telling Rider that he has to share Spring with them."

"Spring loves all the attention Mom. We have been out all day visiting. We went to see his oldest sister, then we ate dinner with Boone's parents so we can eat supper with you and Papa."

"Yes, we have plenty."

"Thanks Mom, set the table and call everybody to eat."

After supper, Kyra and Boone headed home."Boone, today has been a busy Sunday."

"Kyra, put Spring to bed so we can have some alone time." Spring was falling asleep in her dad's arms.

"She is sound asleep, good." The trees were full of snow.

"The season for planting will be upon us soon Kyra. You know this is one of our favorite times of the year," said Boone.

"We can get some plants from Papa this year. Papa has a green thumb for plants," replied Kyra.

"Yes, he is one of the best farmers in this area."

"No, in the world," said Kyra. They both laughed. "Boone, I love you, and our children are a part of the love we share, but we have to connect in more ways than one."

Boone shook his head. "Yes, I know Kyra." Kyra talked until Boone fell asleep.

"Good morning Spring, mommy wants you to wake up for breakfast." Spring rubbed her eyes as she hugged her mom.

"Daddy?" asked Spring.

"Daddy is out feeding the animals, and he will be back soon so you can go with him to get the eggs."

"Boone, Spring is in the bedroom looking for her boots."

"Come here Kyra, he kissed her and hugged her tight, we need a break. I would love to go out this weekend, just you and me. I will ask my mom if Spring can spend Friday night with my sisters.They love to help."

"Okay, sounds good."

Spring walked in with the basket for the eggs, and her favorite boots on the wrong foot.

"Daddy."

"Spring, you are growing up so fast we will have to get you a brother soon." Spring was holding her dad's hand, turning his hand loose and running to the hen house. The chickens were jumping and flying everywhere.

"Spring, wait for me. Put this one in the basket, there is one more. We have them all Spring, I will carry the basket." Spring held on to the side of the basket.

"Mommy mommy," she was showing Kyra the eggs.

"Wow, I can cook eggs for days. Thank you little one for the eggs. Come help me clean the eggs so we can put them in the refrigerator."

Boone took Kyra to Wall Street on Friday night and she had the time of her life. It was a cold night and Kyra was happy.

"I so enjoyed tonight, thanks so much I needed that. I saw so many of our friends. It brought back so many memories of how we fell in love. The owner said he talked to Bubba last month, Bubba is married, with a baby on the way."

"That is good news, that he has his own wife, and not my Kyra." Kyra smiled but said nothing. Kyra sat close to Boone in the truck on the ride home. No words, just good feelings flowing from heart to heart.

"Kyra are you okay?"

"Yea, I just felt a little nauseous."

"You did eat more than the normal."

"Those burgers were so good. Thanks Boone, you welcomed my baby."

# Chapter 22

# Hope for a Son

"Kyra, Lang wrote me a few days ago and she will be home the weekend so plan to spend some time with us," said Philantha.

"Mom, I have been so preoccupied with my life, that I have not written Lang in a few months. She wrote me last and I did not answer. I need some time alone with my sister."

"Married life is not easy, but you do have your family now apart from us, and I understand," said Philantha.

"I miss cooking with you, and helping with Polly and Ammy."

"That is called change Kyra, life never stays the same, always moving forward."

Polly and Ammy were playing with Spring in the next room. Rider and Boe walked in the kitchen with Papa. "Hey Kyra," said Boe.

"Hey, where you all coming from?"

"When the boys came home from school they helped me clean some of my plowing tools that needed to be sharped and shined."

"Rider how was school today?" asked Kyra.

"I am learning additions, and my teacher said, 'I am smart because I can read too."

"Thanks, Boe, because of your great reading skills, you are helping Rider so much. How was your school day?"

"I love school Kyra, every day is a good day for me. Polly came home crying last week after her class had parent teacher day, she wanted her mom."

"I am so glad she will see her mom this weekend," said Kyra.

Tilton said, "Polly did not want me to go, so I asked her if she wanted her Grandmom, the answer was no."

"Times like these are when you realize children need their parents to raise them, and not grandparents. We will do our best as grands and not try to be their parents," replied Philantha.

"I know Lang has regrets but under the circumstances, with wrong choices, it had to end with the girls here with us. They really are happy girls who miss their mom."

"That is true Papa."

Kyra said, "Polly and Ammy love you so much and I believe they will always show that love to you. Just like you said earlier Mom about changes. Boone will not be back to pick me up until late."

"Thanks Mom and Papa, I enjoyed our time together, see you all the weekend."

"How was your day Boone?"

"Busy as always. I helped Dad with repairs on the tractor. We stopped for today, we will finish tomorrow."

"I will warm up leftovers from last night Boone."

"Okay with me. I am hungry Kyra."

Spring jumped up in his lap, hugging her dad's around his neck. Boone asked Spring,"What did you say? Kyra, Spring is talking. Dadda love you," replied Boone. He held Spring tight as tears rolled down his face.

"Why are you crying Boone?"

"Spring just started running and now talking."

Kyra turned her back to Boone with tears in her eyes. "I love you Boone so much."

"Kyra are you okay?" Turning toward Boone she hugged his neck with Spring on the other side. She placed his hand on her stomach. "Kyra, why you did not tell me. You are so small, I could not tell. How far are you?"

"Three months," replied Kyra.

"No, Kyra you can't be that far that means we will have our son by the summer. So, you were pregnant Christmas."

"Yes, but I did not know for sure, and I was so excited about Spring's first birthday party celebration with you. Put Spring in her bed." She had fallen asleep in her dad's lap.

"Boone, I did not know for a few months myself. I knew something was different. I never got sick, so I just pushed the thought aside until a few days ago when I realized my period had not shown again. Are you happy?"

"Happy is not the word Kyra, I will have to plant a double crop this year." They both laughed as they made love and fell asleep.

*****

Lang came back home to visit her family after several months. Everyone was happy about Lang's visit. Kyra was excited to see her sister, she hurried over to talk with Lang.

"Lang, we have so much to catch up on, I have not seen you in months," said Kyra.

"Kyra, I did not recognize Polly nor Ammy, and Rider is a little thick like our mom and her sisters," said Lang.

"Girl, do not let Rider hear you say that about him. Rider is growing into a little gentle boy. Boe is so patient with him, teaching him some principles of life as a young boy," said Kyra.

"Kyra, I think Boe was born a gentleman. Kyra are you ready for another child?"

"I have to be Lang; in a few months I will have my second child. I am excited for Spring to have a sibling. Look at you and I, we will always be close. I am so glad Mom and Papa had you. I love our brothers, but it is nothing like having you, Lang, as my sister."

"Kyra we are so blessed to be sisters, I could never thank you for your love for me and my girls. That's enough about me. How are you and your boyfriend?"

"Kyra, I am in love with him and I think he feels the same. Yes, he could be my husband." Lang's visit ended too soon, as she went back to the city days later. Kyra went home and life returned to normal. Over the months, she kept in touch with Lang about her baby's due date. Kyra wrote a letter telling Lang that the baby would be here any day now. Kyra was home because her time was close to deliver. A few days later, Kyra's water broke as soon as Boone came home from work.

"You can get the midwife Boone." Kyra was sweating Boone was scared as he waited to hear the baby cry. Philantha and Papa came to see the baby boy.

"Kyra, how are you?" asked Philantha.

"I am good but, Mom, I am concerned about the baby. Jabesh, he barely cried when he was born and he is still very quiet. I love Jabesh."

"He knows you love him."

The pain was so great in Boone and Kyra's heart. Kyra and Boone were so hopeful for their son, that Boone desired so much. But the doctors gave them little hope. In six months Jabesh passed. Something died on the inside of them. Life was not the same, but they had Spring to raise and looking forward to having more children. Fear, pain and disappointment were a part of their lives.

"Kyra, I love you, it was not your fault or mine. Somethings we will never understand. We can have more boys and girls."

"They cannot take the place of Jabesh."

"I know Kyra, remember, his name means born in pain, but blessed."

Boone encouraged Kyra daily to read the scripture, *Joel 2:25, "So I will restore to you the years that the locust has eaten."* "Kyra, we will allow these words to bring us healing as we move forward as a family," said Boone.

Jabesh passed before Christmas time, Spring's birthday and Boone's birthday. This is one of the times from which a lot of newlyweds would never recover.

Boone kept encouraging Kyra to read the scripture and get out of the house. One day, Boone was going to town and decided to ask Kyra to come because he felt she had something on her mind.

"Kyra would you like to go with me to town today?"

"No Boone, I am not feeling well," said Kyra.

"What's wrong?"

"I ate breakfast, and it did not agree with my stomach?"

"Kyra you never feel sick, unless."

"Unless what Boone?" asked Kyra.

"You had a period?"

"Not for the month yet, but I should in a few days." Boone waited for Kyra to tell him, if she was with child.

"Kyra, are you pregnant?"

Kyra just cried and said, "I am not ready to have another baby. I am so afraid, scared, and still hurting from the loss of Jabesh."

"We will have to accept this child Kyra just as we did Spring and Jabesh."

"Okay. Boone, I know God will help us."

## Chapter 23

## The Family Grows

"Miles, it is so good to see you. How are you and your friend?"

"I think I will ask her to be my wife."

"So, you are serious?"

"Yes Boone, we enjoy each other in so many ways. I think it is time for me to settle down and have a family in a few years, not right away."

"Maybe Kyra and I will move to the city."

"Wow! I would love that so much, then our kids could grow up together."

"I will talk with Kyra."

"Miles and I are going out on the town tonight and have some brother time okay."

"Sounds good."

"His friend wants to stay with you and the kids. I would love that."

"Goodnight, see you tomorrow, Miles."

Kyra was still up when Boone came home, "Looks like you two enjoyed your time." Boone could only smile as he kissed Kyra, he was feeling tipsy. He almost fell on the chair; Kyra helped him to the bed. Boone fell fast asleep. The next morning, Boone slept late.

"Boone you okay?" asked Kyra.

"Yes, I have a little headache from all the fun we had last night."

"I have some last minute items to bake for the dinner party today. Oh, I invited Lizzie and her son."

"Why Kyra, you know she likes Miles?" asked Boone.

"Lizzie stopped by yesterday and she likes Miles friend too. They talked and it's okay for my cousin to come to dinner."

The dinner party started and everybody was talking and enjoying the music. Lizzie and Hagan arrived at the party and walked over to talk to Kyra and Boone.

"Boone, I need to meet one of your friends," said Lizzie.

"What about Hagan's dad?"

"I need a husband and a full-time dad for Hagan."

"I may have one in mind, but my choice may not be yours, so we will see." Everybody enjoyed the dinner. Lizzie was leaving and Miles walked her to the door.

"How are you Lizzie?"

"Hagan makes me happy. You look happy Miles."

"Yes, I am. Remember we had some great times together, but we never got the love connection. I hope you find your love Lizzie, goodnight." Miles gave her a big hug.

"Good night Miles, take care of yourself and your friend," said Lizzie.

As Miles was leaving, he put the brakes on his brother, "You need more time with Kyra, to build your marriage and enhance your love for her, so that you do not get overwhelmed."

*****

Kyra wrote Lang and shared her news, she talked about how happy she was to see Miles. Lang wrote back and told Kyra she got married and they will be home soon.

"Mom, I am so happy for Lang, she deserves a good man."

"You are right Kyra, don't we all," said Philantha.

The girls asked if he has to be their new daddy. Ammy said, "Papa is my only dad."

Polly added, "I know that's right."

"What did you say Mom?"

"I will leave that up to your mom girls, and yes, Papa is your dad."

Kyra and Boone left from visiting her family and went to visit Boone's family. Boone's mom met them at the door with good news.

"Miles got married Boone; I got a letter yesterday," said Boone's mom.

"Wow! That was fast. All this good news, I love it Mom," said Boone.

"How are you Kyra? It is about time for the birth of your child?"

"I hope it is another boy. Kyra was so concerned this time she asked Boone if she could have a doctor and not a midwife."

"The baby will be just fine, but if that is what you want so be it." As they were talking, Lizzie drove up the road and stopped to chat with Kyra. Kyra and Lizzie stepped away to talk.

"Lizzie, why did you hide your pregnancy from me?"

"You thought I was just fat, Kyra?"

"Yes, you are a little thick."

"Ha Ha funny Kyra."

"I love you Lizzie. Who is the baby daddy? I know it is not Hagan's."

"Leave it there Kyra." Spring ran toward Lizzie. Hagan was trying to catch her.

"Hey little one. Spring saved you Lizzie; we will talk later."

Later that day, Boone and Kyra are home discussing life. Kyra noticed Boone does not talk about his time in the military.

"Boone I was thinking more about your time in the Navy since the 4th of July just passed a few weeks ago. You are always so quiet about those years."

"Kyra, I love my country and all the great men that I became close friends with. We were young men, there for one another, but really scared boys. We were afraid of dying in a battle and drowning at sea. And there was much racial segregation that we experienced. I pray our children will be free to connect and have relationships with any race."

*****

A few days later, Lizzie birthed another healthy baby boy. Hagan now had a baby brother to play with after school. Hagan, Polly, Ammy and Rider all went to the same school, and in two weeks, they would be returning. Kyra was getting close to have her baby. Tilton and Rider arrived at Kyra's house to find her about to go into labor.

"Papa and Rider are here," said Spring.

Kyra was lying across the bed, "Papa, I think I am almost ready."

"Almost?"

"Yes, I have to be very sure because Boone has to get the doctor to come to us this time. The doctor is due for a house call tomorrow. So, we will see what he says, I am uncomfortable, but experiencing no pain. This is my 40th week."

The next day, the doctor arrived and Kyra gave birth to a baby girl. The baby girl was screaming as she came out. "Kyra she is a healthy big baby girl," said the doctor.

Kyra was crying as the doctor placed the baby beside her. Kyra looked at Boone and then the baby. Boone got the placenta in the basin to bury outside and walked the doctor to the door and thanked him for coming.

"Boone, are you sure she looks okay?"

"The doctor said, 'she looks great, and she is so fat.' Do you need anything Kyra?" asked Boone.

"Yes. Some water, I am thirsty after pushing this big girl out."

"Spring, come in to see your sister."

She ran from the next room. Mama pretty," as she kissed the baby.

"What is her name?"

"Omah is her name. Say, Oomah Spring."

"Oom."

"That is close enough for now." Boone was very quiet.

Months passed as Kyra and Boone watched as Omah grow into a quiet little girl that could play well alone. Omah loved to spend time at her Grandmom, Philantha and Papa's house because Boe was her favorite uncle.

Boe said, "She was his baby because she was quiet like him." She grew up watching Philantha sew, cook, and clean. She was also fascinated with the snuff that her Grandmom placed in her bottom lip.

Boone was not good with babies, so he took care of Spring while Kyra took care of Omah majority of the time.

Omah and Spring were very close. Spring was overprotective of her. She followed Spring anywhere. Omah looked to her sister as one would to their mom. Kyra was very affectionate to them. Boone showed more love to Spring for some reason.

"Spring! Omah! Come here, Daddy wants to go to his parents for dinner."

"Yes" said Spring.

"We love to go to Grandmom Dara and Granddad Blair's house to eat and play with our cousins." She took Omah by the hand and they skipped to the car together. Kyra was due with her fourth child soon.

"Kyra, I love farming and raising the girls here, but I would love to move near Miles one day," said Boone.

Kyra said, "I never really thought about the city. Lang always tried to get me to come see her, and I would say not at this time. Boone, I think in a few years but not right now."

"Yes in the future. We will wait until you give birth to this baby. Let's save money from the crops in the next few years, then move. Miles is sure he can help us find housing when we are ready to come. I am excited Kyra."

A week later, Kyra went into labor. "Boone, I am ready to deliver," said Kyra.

"I will get the truck and go get the midwife."

"I will be okay Boone. Yes go now." Boone and the midwife returned and Kyra gave birth to a baby girl.

"We have another baby girl Kyra."

They both said, "We will have a cheering squad before a football team." Omah and Spring were ready to come in the room after they heard the baby crying.

"Mom, another sister? Two sisters, I am so happy," said Spring.

"Her name is Lalla, give her a kiss."

Spring was school age, while Omah and Lalla were home with Kyra. Lalla was quiet and loved to play with Omah in the mud. The girls are growing like weeds.

"Kyra, you dress them so cute, they look like triplets."

"Mom helps me so much with the beautiful dresses she sews for the girls," replied Kyra.

*****

Boone and Kyra discussed their move to the city. "Kyra, I think we have saved enough money to plan to move next year. After the baby is born, we will move in the fall once the baby is old enough to travel. It will be summer, so the oldest girls can start school for the year and not miss any school time."

"Okay Boone, that sounds good. I hope it is the boy that you have been waiting for after losing Jabesh."

"Kyra. I am taking Omah with me to my mom's before Spring gets out of school."

"Okay, Lalla is taking a nap." Boone walked in the yard with Omah, when something moved under his truck.

"Step back Omah."

"What is it Daddy?"

"There is a snake under the truck. I have to kill it before it goes into someone's yard."

"Okay, Dad I am stepping back." Omah stepped back too fast and fell. She was screaming and blood was flowing down her face.

"Omah! Are you okay?" asked Boone as he rushed over to her.

"Daddy, I am scared." Boone picked up Omah and ran into the house.

"Kyra Kyra!! Omah cut her face when she fell in the yard."

"Give her to me Boone. Get me some soot from the heater it will stop the bleeding. Okay baby, you will be okay." Kyra rocked Omah until she stopped crying. Boone was holding Lalla, who woke up from hearing Omah crying.

"Boone you have to go get Spring, I meet her at this time of day."

"I will change my shirt, so I do not scare Spring with all this blood."

"Yes, that was a lot of blood. Thank God the soot stopped the bleeding and that you were almost in the yard."

"Omah wants to go to sleep, but I will have to keep her awake for a while since she had a head injury."

Spring was holding Omah's hand, telling her that she would be alright.

"I was so scared. I saw the dead snake, and Dad hung it in a big tree."

"Kyra, hearing Omah crying with blood all over her face was scary. I need to relax for a moment before I clean the glass from the truck," said Boone.

"Okay," said Kyra.

"Dad I am good, I am not scared when I am with you," said Omah.

"I just want you to be safe," replied Boone. They all hugged and Omah ran in the house to play with Lalla.

# Chapter 24

# Boone and Kyra Move to the City

Boone, we have so much to pack. We have three months, so do not stress yourself because Ollie is just a month old. Our fourth baby girl is a ray of sunshine."

"Kyra I can tell because you are more peaceful."

"Boone, while Spring is in school, Omah helps so much with Lalla and that gives me time to take care of Ollie and the housework."

"I am so excited about our upcoming life together in the city."

"Kyra, I am nervous now just thinking of a public job and having enough income to take care of my family," said Boone.

"Boone it will be a lot, but together we can do it."

"I love you Kyra you are a strong woman, wife, and a great mother to our four daughters."

"Thanks, I love you Boone, always know that it is like a brand tattooed on my heart, Boone's forever."

"Kiss me lady because last night was a night like we had before we had the babies." Ollie started crying and the conversation stopped.

"Spring get your boots and your raincoat."

"I have my boots too," said Omah.

"Okay, you can go with me Omah."

"Mom when will I go to school? I can write my name. I want to be in the same class as Spring." Kyra was a smart mother, she took time to teach the girls how to write their names before they started school.

"Omah, you will be the first one to start school in the city," said Kyra.

Spring added, "Mom, I will help Omah when she goes to school. I know what to do, so she does not have to be afraid." Kyra and the girls arrived at school to drop off Spring.

"Bye Spring," said Omah as she waved.

"Bye Omah. See you later," replied Spring as she went inside.

Later that day, Kyra and Boone were talking while the kids were playing.

Boone said, "Kyra, Miles said it will be another month before I can get the job. He knows the project manager, and she will take a chance with me based on his word. And Kyra, it worked out because the project housing that I will be working for will allow us to live in one of their homes. We will be right next door to Miles and his family. I will be working in a different location, but same company."

"Boone, I am ready with all this good news. Okay, so Ollie will be 5 months old and Omah will be turning 6years old in the same month." Kyra called out, "Spring, Omah get Lalla we are going to my mother's house to tell them our good news." They all went to Philantha's house and told them the good news about the city.

A month passed, Boone's family met at the Tilton's house to say their goodbyes to Kyra and Boone as they made their move to the city. They spent some time talking and then prepared to leave.

"Aunt Kyra, we will miss you and the girls coming over every week. Ammy and I want you to be happy. I will be out of school in a few years and I want to move to the city myself," said Polly.

"Thanks Polly I will always be there for you both." Boe and Rider were happy and sad at the same time, but had girlfriends that occupied their time.

"We will miss you sis, but we want what you want for your life and your family. We will come see you all with Papa," said Boe.

"Mom will you come to see us in the city?" asked Kyra.

"Kyra, you will have to bring the kids to see me. I am a country woman, I like open fields and hot sunny days," replied Philantha.

Tilton said, "Kyra, you know I love to drive, so me and the boys can come and get you and the girls anytime you want to see your mom. I love you all."

Boone kissed his mom, and she would not let him go. Boone was a mama's boy. Spring, Omah, and Lalla were crying, and Ollie was the only one that did not know what was going on. Papa and Boe drove to the city with Boone and Kyra, so that everyone could go at the same time. The drive to the city was fun and exciting for everyone because they were traveling together. A couple of hours later they arrived, and everyone got out the car and headed towards their new home.

"Kyra, I like the housing, the girls can make friends easily in this neighborhood," Boone said after looking around. Omah and Lalla were running up and down the stairs. Spring had Ollie on her hip.

"Girls, Girls!! Please be careful," said Kyra.

"They have never had steps Kyra, and they are wearing them out," said Boone.

"Yes, I am going to wear them out if they do not listen," replied Kyra.

Omah, Lalla and Spring went up the stairs together.

Spring walked upstairs and said, "This is Mom and Dad's room on our right, and this room is for us girls. This last room is for the baby and the babies to come."

Omah said, "I like this bathroom because we can pee and take a bath in the same room. Spring, how do you know about babies?"

Kyra called out come downstairs, "Papa and Boe will be leaving soon. Come say goodbye."

*****

Time passed as they settled into their new home and life. School was about to start for Spring and Omah. The girls were excited to start at their new school.

"Mom I just wanted to write my name."

"You write on paper not my new furniture, Omah."

"Boone it is not funny, but look how good she wrote her name on the dresser top. I have a white cloth dresser liner to cover it up."

"Omah, I have to go with you and Spring to school today to register because both of you are new students. Tomorrow you will go with Spring okay?" Kyra registered them and left. Omah was crying as Kyra left her in the classroom.

"Boone, Omah cries everyday Spring drops her off for her class. She has to get over being scared and nervous," said Kyra.

"She will be okay," replied Boone.

"Ollie is crawling everywhere now. She got past me today and I caught her looking down the stairs. I have to keep this busy one downstairs. Enough about the kids, how was your day at work?"

"Very busy, it seems as if every tenant had a problem today. But we have slow days, so I will not complain. I like my job; I have met a lot of friendly people. I met a Pastor that has bible study with some of the men I work with in his home. I plan to join them next week."

"Sounds good Boone, dinner is almost ready." The girls were outside on the stoop playing with some friends.

"Boone, life here is good. But we can be so busy with life that we overlook each other's needs," said Kyra. As they were talking, the children could be heard upstairs.

"Lalla and Omah, get off the bed!" yelled Spring.

"No Spring! You are not our mom," said Omah.

"Lalla stop copying Omah. Mom told me to get you two off the bed, She can hear you downstairs." Spring tried to grab them off the bed.

"Spring stop!" said Omah.

"No, get down," replied Spring, as she reached for them again. Omah and Lalla ran downstairs crying.

"Mom, Spring hit us, look."

"Spring, do not hit them anymore."

"Mom, they would not listen"

"Okay I will take care of them."

"Hey, what is all the fussing?" Boone said as he walked in and went straight to the pantry after placing his lunch pail on the table.

Omah looked at Kyra and said, "Mom when you go in the pantry you come out with food. And when Dad goes in the pantry, he comes out with nothing, why?"

"Omah grown folk business, go play."

# Chapter 25

# City Life

"Mom, I am going to Connie's house; she wants me to stay tomorrow night. We will have a school break in a few weeks," said Omah.

"Yes, and then you will not want to come home at all," said Kyra.

"Lalla and Ollie love to make mud cakes together and Spring is with her friends, so I have Connie."

"Uncle Miles will bring his daughter, Kallee, to play with us and I will watch her," said Lalla.

"I will take care of Ollie; I am a big girl now," said Omah. Miles son, Jay, brought his sister Kallee outside to play with the girls.

"Boys do not enjoy making mud cakes for dolls to eat. We can play games later, Cousin Lalla when Dad makes some ice cream for us all later today," said Jay.

Later that day, Miles was talking to Boone, who seemed to be quieter than usual. After playing outside with the kids, they all got ice cream. Miles began to talk to Boone about what was bothering him.

"Boone, are you okay? Have you been spending too much time playing cards at the lady's house? You have been very quiet, I told you she was nothing but trouble. I even told Kyra how she broke up so many families. What are you going to do now?" asked Miles.

"Not sure Miles, it is like I am being pulled in half," said Boone who was still in deep thought. Boone never discussed what was on his mind with Miles.

The next morning, Boone overslept after a night out with the guys playing cards.

"Boone, get up, you will be late for your eye examine," said Kyra

"Kyra, okay I was tired."

"I guess so, you got home this morning around 1:00 am. Where were you Boone?"

"Kyra I was with Miles and some of the guys drinking and playing cards."

"You have been drinking more. The kids know why you go in the pantry now Boone," said Kyra.

"But Kyra, they do not see me drinking, so they will not know unless you tell them."

"Omah, was crying when you closed the door to the bathroom this morning and she could not see the light. You know she is afraid of the dark. I am not sure why she woke up. Omah is a very light sleeper; sometimes I think she can sense things in her sleep. She asks me questions that Spring as the oldest never asked."

"See you when you get back Boone, do not forget to get the hot dog rolls when you stop at the grocery store."

Boone returns home with the bread, and greets his family in the kitchen. Kyra and the girls are planning a trip home to see Philantha and Tilton.

"Boone, Papa will pick me and the girls up so we can go see Mom this Friday afternoon early. We will be back Sunday because Monday is a holiday. I am so glad the girls are small because if I have one more child, we will not have the space in the car with Papa and Boe"

"Kyra, we have to have more sons, for sure."

A few days later, Tilton arrived and drove them back to the family's farm in the country. When they arrived at the house, Philantha was happy to see Kyra and the children.

"Ammy, how are you since Polly moved to the city?" asked Kyra.

"I am glad Polly graduated, but I miss her so much Aunt Kyra."

"Polly is working as a waitress just like Mom. I have a few years to decide what I want to do after high school."

"Kyra, Ammy is so in love, I am not sure what her plans are after school," said Philantha.

"Grandmom, why did you tell Aunt Kyra that I like this young man? He will be going away to college when he graduates. We both love basketball and play for our high school teams."

"Sounds great Ammy, Rider told me you were a good basketball player because he taught you all his good moves in the yard."

"Rider and I play one-on-one in the yard, and he really does help me with my game," said Ammy.

Spring was on Rider's lap, and Omah was on Boe's lap. Lalla and Ollie were not leaving Kyra's side. Ollie smiled as Philantha reached out to take her from Kyra's lap. Then Lalla allowed Ammy to hold her.

"Kyra, you have 4 sweet girls. They have their own individuality at their young age in so many ways."

"Yes Mom, they are and Omah is the most helpful one she is a nurturer."

Philantha felt that the visit was too short as they all waved at the car disappearing down the path. Tilton drove as the kids waved from the back window.

"Omah, I thought you were sleep."

"No Mom, I was watching the moon. I was asleep but when I woke up the moon was following us, and it is still following us. As Papa drives fast, the moon seems to go faster. The moon gives me joy it makes me smile." Ollie woke up and Kyra fed her.

"Papa, Omah fell back to sleep with the girls," said Kyra.

"Kyra, we are almost at your house, the sun is coming up now."

"Since you drove all night, please stay until tomorrow. Boe wants to spend some time with Boone."

"Kyra, farm work has no holidays. Boe will drive back this evening. I slept earlier before we left, to bring you home at 4:00 am."

Boone came to the car to get the girls out of the car and put them to bed. "Hey all the girls are sound asleep, and hopefully they will sleep for a few more hours. Maybe until around 10:00, it is 7am now. Papa, you can lay on my bed."

"No Kyra, I will be okay right here on the couch."

"I will cook breakfast since Ollie is asleep too."

"Boe and I will go out back on the stoop until breakfast is ready Kyra."

"Kyra, I like your home. How is the neighborhood?"

"You know Miles and his family are on the right of us, and the family on the left is very kind. So far, it seems to be a very close community of people. The girls have close friends already. I feel safe with them playing outside with their friends."

"Breakfast was good Kyra, look who is up already, Omah."

"Hey Daddy, I missed you."

"I missed you too," said Boone.

"So glad we stayed for dinner Kyra, but it is time to go home. We should be home around 6:00. Boe is driving I am taking a nap," said Tilton.

"Everybody, get ready for your picture before we leave. Look at me and smile," said Boe.

"Uncle, I am glad we can see the picture so quickly."

"Yes Omah, this is a Polaroid camera."

"I want to be a photographer one day myself."

"Sounds good Omah."

"Uncle you took a picture of me, with a lemon in my mouth. I will look back one day at our family picture and ask myself why? Ollie will wonder if she even has on any clothes. Because the only thing we can see is her naked tummy."

"Bye Papa and Boe, love you, safe travels." They all waved as Tilton and Boe drove off. Then they went inside and Kyra began talking to Boone. "Boone, the trip was short, but I was glad to see my mother and she was excited to see Ollie walking for the first time.

"I missed you and the girls; I am glad you all are home and I had time with Boe before he left. I had a good conversation with Boe, he is a good listener."

*****

Time passed and the stress of life began to interfere with Kyra and Boone's marriage. Boone spent the majority of his time away from home working overtime. One day, Boone pulls Miles aside to talk about his troubles.

"Miles, Kyra and I had a bad argument last night. I was out late last night playing cards and drinking," said Boone.

"Boone what is the problem. Are you happy?"

"Yes. I am. I love Kyra, but I also enjoy the excitement of drinking and being with the boys."

"But Kyra needs more attention than you are giving her, the kids take most of her time, that is not easy for her, Boone," said Miles.

"We can have a family gathering Saturday out back with your family and mine. I will ask the ladies to get the food together."

# Chapter 26
# Tension Builds Between Kyra and Boone

"Kyra how are you feeling?"

"The doctor said I have to go on bed rest if I want to carry this child full term."

"Are you ready to go home?" asked Boone.

"Yes, but I have to get a vitamin prescription, the nurse is getting it for me, then we can leave. Boone, I have two more months until my due date this will not be easy. I cannot even go down stairs to cook. I am so glad Ollie is three, Spring and Omah are so good with helping take care of the younger kids. Ollie is so concerned for me, she is in my room every moment asking me if I need anything."

"I'm glad you have the kids to help out while I'm at work," replied Boone.

The next day, Kyra calls to Spring. "Spring I need you and Omah to go to the corner store," Kyra said. Then Boone walked in the house. "Mom, Dad is downstairs, maybe he has already shopped for grocery."

"Girls come put the food away for me, I have to check on your mom." He walked upstairs to check on Kyra. "I have to go back to work. I stopped at the grocery store to buy some food, then I came home to check on you and the girls."

"Okay Boone. Can you make sure that Omah does not burn the rice? They have to finish homework and prepare for school tomorrow." Boone helped the girls before he went back to work. Once he finished working, he and Kyra helped the girls finish their homework.

"Goodnight girls say your prayers."

"Goodnight Mom okay."

*****

Two months passed, it was time for Kyra to give birth.

Kyra woke up in pain, "Boone, I am ready to go to the hospital."

"I will help you into the car and then put Ollie in the back with you." Boone rushed Kyra to the hospital, where he then waited to hear from the doctors.

"Mr. Boone you have a baby boy. You can go in to see your wife," said the doctor.

"Kyra, we have another son," said Boone as he held Kyra's hand as tears rolled down her face.

"Yes Manon, was wished for and our desire has been fulfilled."

"Get some rest while you can and I will stop by the nursery on my way out."

"Boone, I will see you tomorrow."

"I will get someone to keep the girls Kyra so I can come early." Boone left the hospital went home to tell the children that they have a baby brother.

"Girls, I took your mom to the hospital to have the baby and guess what? You have a baby brother, his name is Manon."

"We cannot wait to see him Dad. How is Mom?"

"You know your mom girls, she wants to be home, but she needs rest. And she can get rest while the nurse takes care of the baby for a few days. Girls I am so glad it is the last week of school for the summer vacation, Manon came at a great time of the year."

"Spring, I am glad we have a little brother; maybe Dad will be happy now."

"Right Omah, he talks about losing Jabesh so now he has another son."

"Dad who are we staying with?"

"A friend of mine, she will feed you all before I come back to pick y'all up. Lalla, take Ollie by the hand."

"Come on Ollie I will help you in the house while Dad gets the bags."

"Omah, the lady told Daddy we can go outside with her daughter, and she will watch Lalla and Ollie," Spring said.

A few days later Kyra returns home with baby, Manon.

"Mom, we missed you so much," said Omah.

"Boone, hold the baby so I can get Ollie. I am more than happy to be home too Omah," said Kyra.

"Mom, I was uncomfortable at that ladies house," said Omah as Spring pushed Omah in the side.

"Spring it's okay let her finish," said Kyra.

"But Mom she was nice, she fed us spaghetti and we went outside with her daughter to a party next door," replied Spring.

"Boone, who was the lady the girls were with?"

"Kyra she is the lady that has the card parties for the guys, her husband is always there too."

The next few months passed quickly and summer was fun for the girls playing with their friends on the front lawn and eating homemade ice cream with their Uncle Miles and his family. Manon was crawling everywhere. Ollie ran to get him out of the trash in the pantry.

"Mom, I did not see him, I just heard a noise in the pantry," said Ollie as Kyra and Omah walked into the kitchen.

"Mom, can I spend the night with Connie this weekend? Her mom has to work late, and she asked if I would stay with your approval."

"Omah, what was the reason last week?" asked Kyra.

"Oh, Mom you know Connie is my best friend and I love being with her all the time," replied Omah.

"You are getting older, and I do trust you staying with the Tibbs."

"Mom, I have rehearsal at church for the Christmas play. We will walk with our friends; we need to use Ollie's baby doll for the play. He has ink all over his face, and we will cover that side with the blanket," said Omah.

Kyra asked, "Omah, did Connie say why she can't come to the play?"

"She is Catholic, they only attend mass. Mom, I love Christmas and I am excited to see what I will get this year. Spring, I saw the sheet covering and I think that our gifts are behind the couch," said Omah

"Omah, do not tell Ollie," replied Spring.

"Well, Lalla was with me when I saw the gifts this year. Right Lalla?"

Lalla answered, "Yes, Omah you made me look."

"Omah you are always looking for something hidden or something that you do not need to know," said Kyra.

"I am not sure why, but it is this pulling toward the unknown," said Omah.

"Just like you found the liquor bottles in the pantry," added Spring.

Omah replied, "Mom asked me to get some oatmeal and there was a cloth over in the corner and under the cloth was the bottle. The pulling said remove the cloth Omah, and I did."

*****

As the year passed by, Boone and Kyra are talking about how fast Manon had grown. "Manon is running he is so active Kyra."

"Yes Boone, he keeps me on my toes."

"Can you take him to the bathroom he is doing well with Potty training?"

"Good boy Manon, that's a big boy."

"Yes Dada."

Omah walked in to talk with Kyra and Boone about the family going to the Christmas play. "Mom we would love for you to come with us to the Christmas play."

"I will think about it Omah. Dinner is ready come set the table girls. Boone, I think I am going to see the Christmas play with the girls."

"Are you taking Manon?" asked Boone.

"Please Mom, he will like the play too, they always give peppermint sticks to everyone that comes to the play," Omah added.

"Ok Omah, we will all go together," said Kyra.

"How about you Dad?"

"Maybe the next time, okay."

"Before we go to the Christmas play, write your name on your shoe box and place them down stairs in the living room, so Santa Claus will not get your presents mixed up with someone else's," said Kyra.

"Mom, we wrote our names last week, and I helped Ollie and Manon with their name."

"Thanks Spring."

The next morning, Christmas Day, the kids woke up early to see what Santa had left under the tree.

"Run Lalla," said Omah. Spring had Ollie by the hand so she would not get knocked down as they all ran down stairs. They quickly opened their presents. Manon was so happy playing with his truck.

"Look what Santa gave me Mom!" said Ollie.

"Wow! Glad you all love your presents," said Kyra. The kids thanked their mom and dad for the gifts. The family discussed the coming of the new baby while playing with Christmas gifts.

"Mom, I am so glad you did not have to be in the bed with this baby," said Omah.

"Yes Omah, thank God I only have a few weeks, so we have to prepare now."

"I want another sister and Spring wants a brother; we talked about it last week."

Weeks passed and Kyra went into labor. Boone drove her to the hospital. "Boone, you cannot bring all the kids with you to the hospital. Who can you get to watch them for a few hours?"

"The same lady I asked to watch them last time," replied Boone. After Kyra gave birth to a baby girl, Boone leaves to check on the kids.

"Children, Mom had another little girl, we named her Olianna."

"Where are we going Dad?"

"I want you all to stay with my friend until I visit Mom at the hospital. She will feed you all before I come back to pick you up."

"Ollie take Manon's hand," said Spring.

"Lalla and Omah will get the bag that Dad has with the changing clothes."

"Omah we will be good, remember this is the same house when Manon was born."

"I will tell Mom again Spring," said Omah.

"I know you will, Omah."

Boone brought Kyra and baby Olianna home. The children were happy to see their sister.

"Where did you all stay, Omah?" asked Kyra. Spring pushed Omah in the side. "Spring, it's alright I just want to know where you all were staying."

"The same lady Mom, she fed us again.

Omah was excited to discuss her babysitting job with Kyra. "Mom, I will start babysitting this week from four until eight. Their mom plans to start her new job. She likes the city better than the country. The boy is four and the little girl will be three soon. Mom they are sweet little kids."

"Omah, be sure to finish your homework as you take care of the kids."

"I will Mom. Get some rest, see you later."

"Olianna is the prettiest little girl, with them puppy eyes. I think Manon is finally realizing Olianna will be staying here with us."

"Mom, Connie wants to see Olianna. When can she come over to visit?" asked Omah.

"Soon," replied Kyra.

"Thanks Mom, I will tell her." Weeks passed and Connie came over to see Olianna.

"Omah, she is pretty, I cannot wait until this summer when we can take her outside," said Connie.

"Mom, I am going to walk Connie halfway home I will be right back."

## Chapter 27

# Love Always Wins

March had approached, the month known for all kinds of weather changes. As Kyra looked out the window at the snow and maybe sleet falling, she decided to write a letter to Lang. She began by telling her how much she was missed, and they had so much to talk about. Kyra ended the letter with hope to see you soon, love Kyra.

*****

As the years passed, the pressures of every day challenges got in the way of Kyra and Boone expressing their love for each other. Deep down they loved each other, but money, job and kids became the center point of the marriage. For love to be affective it has to be fed.

Boone started staying away from home more often. Kyra knew things were changing in her life and eventually she would have to adjust to the change. When changes come, we have to embrace our change, accept our change, and move forward through the pain, hurt and disappointments. She had to make a positive move forward without Boone in order to take care of herself and the children. She assured them that everything they had built together and desired as a family must continue. Although, Boone was not present in the home anymore, his love and memory would always be cherished in the family. Kyra's faith in God gave her strength to move back to the country with her family. Being a woman of faith, she knew God would always provide for her family. Kyra moved back to the country with her six children, ages from 2 to 16 years old. It was after returning back to her parents, Kyra found out she was just two months pregnant with her seventh child. She had a son and named him Nixon, meaning overcomer, which helped Kyra to overcome her loss of Boone. In the midst of her pain, she still had pleasure knowing the right decision was made to keep the family moving forward.

*The children she and Boone conceived in their love connection would* ***always be in her tender heart.***

## *TO MY CHILDREN WORDS OF WISDOM*

*"Children in life we are faced with unexpected challenges. We must understand pain and joy. Why hate and not love? The bible tells us that there is a time and a season for everything under the sun. We will get through this season together. Remember and never forget that "Love Always Win."*

## *-The End-*

# *About The Author*

Dolphine Solomon Lynch is a born dreamer who has a great imagination. She expresses her thoughts through writing and journaling. Dolphine has a great love for family. A wife, mother, grandmother, business partner with her husband.

Dolphine is a storyteller at heart, which some people would never know. Her siblings call her the comedian with wisdom. She believes that no one should ever stop dreaming because dreams do come true. Her hobbies include portrait painting and crafting. Dolphine is a writer who will open the eyes and ears of many as she broadens their imagination through novels

Wall street Lady is her first novel with more to come.

www.ingramcontent.com/pod-product-compliance
Lightning Source LLC
Chambersburg PA
CBHW021427070526
44577CB00001B/101